In Praise of *Sentness*

"The word *missional* is in danger of becoming a vacuous trend in twenty-first-century evangelicalism, claiming to be new wine but packaged and consumed in the same old programmatic wineskins. This is why we need *Sentness*. Hammond and Cronshaw pull back the curtain on what *missional* really means and help us conceive the new wineskins (postures and practices, not programs) that are needed to hold this missional wine that looks new but is actually very old and very powerful. What is needed is not more tips, techniques, buzz words and events—what is needed are new ways of being human together that show and tell the power of the gospel of Jesus Christ. Hammond and Cronshaw—drawing from their deep well of experience—describe our way forward as a sent people into the missional frontier of North America."
Mike Breen, CEO, 3DM

"Austrian philosopher Ivan Illich once remarked that the best way to change society is by telling an alternative story. Kim Hammond and Darren Cronshaw do this masterfully in *Sentness*. By relating inspiring examples of ordinary people who are simply but effectively impacting their communities for Christ, they encourage anyone with a desire for incarnational mission to say, 'I could do that!'"
Felicity Dale, author, *An Army of Ordinary People*

"Could it be that while much of the church is waiting for Jesus to come, Jesus is waiting for us to go? This book joins a chorus of voices calling for the church to join God on mission in our world with lots of practical ideas as to how we can do so more effectively. Highly recommended reading."
Mark Conner, CityLife Church, Australia

"*Sentness* weaves solid theology with thoughtful praxis to not only remind us that all Christ-followers are sent but also to show us how to live a sent life. Hammond and Cronshaw are two leaders who not only teach it but personally live it out, and that is reflected in this great book. If the church will embrace the six postures in *Sentness* the mission of Jesus will be accomplished!"
Dave Ferguson, coauthor, *Exponential*

"*Sentness* is a fast-paced and inspiring invitation. It will challenge you to place your home, neighborhood and job under the direction of Jesus and cause you to rethink concepts of church, ministry and mission. It is time to respond to the invitation to be sent—this book is an essential guide."

Geoff Maddock, urban missionary

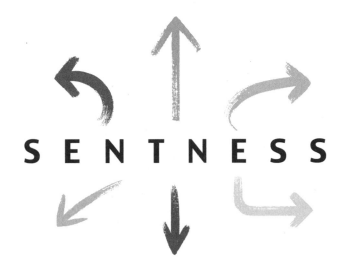

S E N T N E S S

SIX POSTURES OF
MISSIONAL CHRISTIANS

KIM HAMMOND
DARREN CRONSHAW

Foreword by Michael Frost and Alan Hirsch

IVP Books

An imprint of InterVarsity Press
Downers Grove, Illinois

InterVarsity Press
P.O. Box 1400, Downers Grove, IL 60515-1426
World Wide Web: www.ivpress.com
Email: email@ivpress.com

InterVarsity Press® is the book-publishing division of InterVarsity Christian Fellowship/USA®, a movement of students and faculty active on campus at hundreds of universities, colleges and schools of nursing in the United States of America, and a member movement of the International Fellowship of Evangelical Students. For information about local and regional activities, write Public Relations Dept., InterVarsity Christian Fellowship/USA, 6400 Schroeder Rd., P.O. Box 7895, Madison, WI 53707-7895, or visit the IVCF website at www.intervarsity.org.

Unless otherwise indicated, all Scripture quotations are taken from the Holy Bible, New Living Translation, copyright ©1996, 2004, 2007. Used by permission of Tyndale House Publishers, Inc., Wheaton, Illinois 60189. All rights reserved.

While all stories in this book are true, some names and identifying information in this book have been changed to protect the privacy of the individuals involved.

Cover design: Cindy Kiple
Interior design: Beth Hagenberg
Image: arrows: ©ulimi/iStockphoto

ISBN 978-0-8308-4418-0 (print)
ISBN 978-0-8308-8406-3 (digital)

Printed in the United States of America

green
press
INITIATIVE   InterVarsity Press is committed to protecting the environment and to the responsible use of natural resources. As a member of Green Press Initiative we use recycled paper whenever possible. To learn more about the Green Press Initiative, visit www.greenpressinitiative.org.

Library of Congress Cataloging-in-Publication Data

Hammond, Kim, 1974-
   Sentness : six postures of missional Christians / Kim Hammond and Darren Cronshaw.
      pages cm
   Includes bibliographical references.
   ISBN 978-0-8308-4418-0 (pbk. : alk. paper)
1. Mission of the church. 2. Church. 3. Missions—Theory. 4. Missional church movement. I. Title.
   BV601.8.H3556 2014
266—dc23

                                                                        2013047715

P	18	17	16	15	14	13	12	11	10	9	8	7	6	5	4	3	2	1
Y	29	28	27	26	25	24	23	22	21	20	19	18	17	16	15	14			

CONTENTS

FOREWORD

EVERY ONE OF US on the missional journey can tell of the shifts we've gone through to move from safe, conventional church models to the radical, incarnational, immersed approach we now take. Some of us took those shifts enthusiastically, diving in with real gusto and excitement. Others took more tentative steps, carefully letting go of the old and slowly taking hold of the new. Others still will have only just begun to embrace the seismic shifts required to become truly missional.

No matter where you find yourself on this journey or how long it's taken for you to get here, we think you'll find that Kim Hammond and Darren Cronshaw beautifully describe what you've been through and what is still in store for you. That's because they aren't merely armchair missiologists—they're local practitioners, living out the very things they're asking of you, their readers. They've been through these shifts themselves, and we all do well to pay attention to what they're saying.

It has been observed that when it comes to making such shifts in thinking and action people will move through four distinct stages:

1. *Unconscious incompetence.* People in this stage are simply not aware of the issue at hand; they are incompetent and they don't even

know it. At this stage, the leader's task is to raise awareness so the learning process can begin. At the very least this involves *selling the problem* before suggesting possible solutions and ways forward. Why? Because we know that the vast majority of people have to first experience some level of frustration in their actions or a significant disruption in their lives (individual or corporate) before they will change. At this stage holy discontent, accompanied by an imaginative search for answers, will move people toward the changes necessary to them participating fully in God's mission. If you've picked this book up, the chances are you've moved beyond this stage.

2. *Conscious incompetence.* Here the learner becomes aware of the issue but at the same time becomes aware of their own relative incompetence in adequately "doing it." So the learner has to decisively push beyond the pressure from their prevailing understandings (which feel very comfortable and natural) and learn to live with significant discomfort and anomaly. This stage involves significant amounts of *unlearning*—even repentance where necessary—in order to move on. Clearly, practicing the new ideas will feel unnatural at this point. It is critical not to simply retreat to what we know. Courage, vision and determination are important.

3. *Conscious competence.* This phase happens when people understand the basic dynamics of the new paradigm but still need to concentrate in order to operate well; it is not *yet* second nature or automatic. Like a new driver, navigating the road takes concentration and practice, but the natural reflexes will come. The slogan "Practice makes perfect" might well apply here, until the final phase eventually comes.

4. *Unconscious competence.* Here the paradigm becomes instinctual; it is hard to see reality any other way. Those at this stage are true insiders of the paradigm and are now competent to teach others about what they themselves have learned and integrated.

We find that this categorization provides us with a way of assessing the progress of missional church thinking over the last decade or so. Certainly there has been an adoption of the basic ideas of missional church by our best and most progressive leaders, but in our opinion, as a whole, the evangelical church is likely transitioning somewhere between conscious incompetence (stage 2) and conscious competence (stage 3). Praise God, there is a definite movement going on. But if we are being honest, it still doesn't come that easily. The movement toward sentness is going to take more practice—in both *thinking* and *acting* differently—before a missional understanding of church becomes second nature.

We need guides who can lead us to competence and good instincts. We can heartily recommend Kim and Darren to you for this journey because they know what it means to be sent. Drawing on their involvement in the Forge Mission Training Network, as well as their unique localized missionary practice, in *Sentness* they tell stories, further develop missiological concepts and suggest various methodologies that are working in various places. The six postures in this book cover a full range of missional thinking, including a distillation of the very best theological work around. But Kim and Darren also anchor such thinking in story, images, advice and examples that bring the ideas to life. It is because of all this that they are well-equipped to help Christians and churches through the clunky transition from missional incompetence to competence.

In his classic tale *Watership Down*, Richard Adams tells the story of Fiver, a nervous little rabbit who develops a messianic hunch that something terrible is going to happen to his Sandleford warren. Fiver tells his brother Hazel, and they try to warn the other rabbits without success. Marginalized as doomsayers, Fiver and Hazel decide they must leave anyway. They are joined by a small band of followers even as their warren is destroyed by a housing developer's bulldozers. There is now no turning back.

So the little band takes off across the countryside in search of a new home. As they make their escape they court many great dangers. They must cross a stream, traverse a bean field and negotiate an open road. These are obstacles that rabbits normally never encounter, and in such situations everything within the DNA of a rabbit tells it to stop running, to dig deep into the cool, cool earth. For Fiver and Hazel and their band to continue across the fox-infested open fields, they must countermand their every natural impulse. How are they to do it?

The answer lies in a surprising quarter. Whenever the rabbits are confronted by a challenge, they stop and rehearse the stories of their folk hero, the prince with a thousand enemies. The stories these rabbits tell and retell themselves unite the band and fill them with courage; they provide answers for the dilemmas posed by life on the road. The rabbits become a story-formed community, and those stories spur them on, driving them forward to the safety of Watership Down.

Think of Kim and Darren as our Fiver and Hazel. They have intuited the need for radical change and led us out across the open fields. And they know the stories that will shape us and remake us into the missional people of God we were intended to be in the first place. Wherever you are on this journey, they are safe, challenging, inspiring guides for the road ahead.

Michael Frost and Alan Hirsch
coauthors, *The Shaping of Things to Come*
cofounders, Forge Mission Training Network

INTRODUCTION

Shift

$\curvearrowright$

Anyone with ears to hear must listen to the Spirit and
understand what he is saying to the churches.

REVELATION 2:7

Mission was understood as being derived from the very nature of God
. . . Father, Son, and Holy Spirit sending the church into the world . . .
a movement from God to the world; the church is viewed as an
instrument for that mission. . . . There is a church
because there is a mission, not vice versa.

DAVID BOSCH

THERE ARE TWO COMPETING POSTURES for the people of God
today: a church of consumers, demanding goods and services, and
a church of missionaries, sent and sending into the world. These
compete for the minds of Christians. Every church functions ac-

cording to one or the other. Every disciple stands on these two foundations for life, two theological bases for making decisions, two postures that shape all we do: selling or sending. We have come to realize that too often and in too many ways the church has been selling when we should be embracing our sentness.

This book will explore these two very different postures and give you some practical ways to break away from the things holding you back from living in fullness and sentness.

We are convinced the biggest issue facing the church today is that we have bought deeply into consumer church. The greatest opportunity for the church is to shift from selling to sending by adopting the posture of sentness.

THE REVOLUTION WILL NOT BE TELEVISED

This is a shift that is happening subversively at all sorts of exciting grassroots levels. It is a movement that has the potential to change not just how we *do* church, but how we *be* the church in the world. And yet this is not a new program or product. In fact, it is a return to the foundational mission-focused DNA of the church that Jesus unleashed on the world.

Singer Gil Scott-Heron's song "The Revolution Will Not Be Televised" sent the provocative message in 1970 that social revolution is not something we can ignore, like a television show we can tune out. In the midst of massive struggles for racial equality and justice for fellow African Americans, Scott-Heron was inviting his listeners to believe in, and work for, new ways of seeing and living in the world. Revolution is not something that offers easy fixes or tantalizing pleasures. It does not filter down to a thirty-second news snippet. Revolution doesn't address annoying inconveniences; it addresses destructive patterns in the world that we have the opportunity to bring to an end. As Scott-Heron put it, "The revolution will not fight the germs that may cause bad breath; the revolution *will* put you in the driver's seat."

Scott-Heron saw the song as being "about your mind."

> You have to change your mind before you change the way you live and the way you move. . . . The thing that's going to change people will be something that no one will ever be able to capture on film. It will just be something you see and all of a sudden you realize "I'm on the wrong page, or I'm on the right page but I'm on the wrong note. And I've got to get in sync with everyone else to understand what is happening."[1]

Sentness is the same way. The word *missional* may be dismissed by some as a trend in contemporary church culture. But like any social movement or revolution, sentness can't be trivialized by television, substituted by pleasure, downgraded by consumerism or delegated to a sermon or Bible study series. We are convinced that our missional sentness cannot be commercialized, regulated or domesticated. The Christian Industrial Complex cannot buy it, sell it or make it into a ride. There will be no novelty toy with a *Sentness* boxed lunch. Those who are a part of Jesus' mission—this holy revolution of sentness—will not be telemarketed to. True missional communities read the Gospels not as bedtime tales but as dangerous stories to be lived out in communities that share life and common mission. Our commitment to sentness and our relationships hold the missional tribe together.

Hundreds of thousands of people have bravely started to use words for the holy dissatisfaction they feel with a church characterized by consumerism. They are not antichurch; they simply are the church. We are convinced that in the future we will talk about this period in church history as a reawakening of the church to incarnational mission. It will be seen as a time when the conversation changed and the people of God acted with new imagination.

Maybe you feel the same way. You may have long realized the importance of mission. Or you may have recently had your imagination captured by what God is doing in the world. It is exciting to be a part of this historic time and to play a small part in this worldwide phenomenon.

The rediscovery of our identity as "missional church" is capturing the imagination of believers around the world. Authors write about it. Conference speakers talk about it. Seminaries teach about it. Thousands of people blog about it. We want to encourage you to live it and to teach others to do the same.

This book is meant to help you imagine missional life for you and for those God has called you into community with. It is our prayer that the people of God will be unleashed from prevailing models and programs to become mapmakers for the future. We hope this book will help you mentor, motivate and mobilize others to be sent into all sorts of dangerous expressions of the kingdom. We pray the imagination of your community will be grabbed by a vision of sentness, and you and your friends will break the bonds of consumer Christianity. We hope you will stand on the shoulders of the history and heritage of the denomination, church or faith you know, and see your way to a new and fresh season of mission. We trust you will embrace your sentness not just in a theoretical paradigm shift, but in your ordinary, everyday life, so that you will bravely do extraordinary things for Jesus and the kingdom of God.

THE BOTH-AND BOOMERANG

The foundations of sentness, outlined in the chapters of this book, are what we have learned over the years as we've pastored local churches and as we've trained local missionaries and church leaders. In the 1990s, I (Kim) was working as a youth pastor at South Eastern Christian Centre, a Pentecostal charismatic church in Melbourne, Australia. At its biggest, South Eastern had over a thousand members. People criticize Pentecostals, but we were good people. We didn't hold snakes and do weird things in our services, although we did like to push people over when we prayed for them. (During prayer times, I was assigned to catch people who fell over.) We loved when the Spirit came; we loved to see people fall over. We loved to collect offerings.

We also loved evangelism. I can remember, as a kid, going out to the local market on Saturday mornings to hand out tracts and tell people about Jesus. The center of everything, however, was Sunday. Sunday was the big show, the main deal. Most of our conversions happened on Sunday.

Very few people have heard of South Eastern Christian Centre (or CRC Churches International, the Australia-based denomination I'm ordained in), but they are my family. South Eastern Christian Centre was the only church community I had ever belonged to and the only style of church I had ever experienced. I was a poor kid from the local area. I remember praying the sinner's prayer and giving my life to Jesus when my dad left us in the middle of the night and a friend of my mom's came to our house and shared the gospel with us.

I met my wife, Maria, in the youth group at South Eastern. She was one of the pastor's kids. I graduated high school, went to a local seminary called Tabor College, and the next thing I knew the church offered me a part-time staff position. I'm sure marrying one of the pastor's daughters wasn't a deciding factor in my getting hired, but I doubt it hurt.

I was the small-groups pastor for the entire church, including the young people. The National Church Life Survey at the time said Australian churches were retaining less than 7 percent of young adults (eighteen to thirty-five years old).[2] Maria and I loved having young people in our home, but we were concerned: Where were all those young people going? Why were they leaving the church and, in most cases, their faith?

We decided to join our lifelong mentors, youth pastors and family friends, Steve and Sonia Swain, in leading a church plant we were calling The Junction. This meant resigning as paid staff at the church I had grown up in. It also meant asking tough questions about how to translate the gospel to people who had walked away from the church. We really wanted to reach people who would not walk through the front door of a church.

Back at Tabor College, finishing my ministry degree, I told one of my close friends, Warwick Vincent, "I think we are going to plant a church."

"What kind of church?" he asked. "A big one or a little one?"

That is almost an offensive question to a Pentecostal. "Of course a big one," I said.

"How big?"

I said as humbly as I could muster, "I don't know—one or two thousand people?"

Warwick didn't look impressed. Then he said something that would change my perspective of ministry and mission forever: "What if God wants you to have lots of little churches? What if God wants you to plant fifty churches of twenty people each?"

Little was not a word in my vocabulary. I had no idea what he was talking about. I had never heard of house churches or missional churches. My brain began to race.

Warwick encouraged me to connect with Alan Hirsch and Forge Mission Training Network. So, in that one conversation, he had introduced me to a whole new paradigm for church and mission.

I had received comprehensive training in big-church practices. I had been a trainee pastor and local church pastor for four years. I had been nationally credentialed and ordained as a pastor in my denomination. I *love* my heritage. I *love* the local church where I was taught. But I was also painfully aware I had lost touch with my neighbors and friends who were not followers of Jesus.

After nine months of transition and finishing at South Eastern, we moved and gathered a dozen friends who were going to form our core church-planting team. We honored the agreement to wait another six months before we held public services. I was fine with that, because it allowed me to take a break from church as we had known it, while I went off to my first intensive training course with Forge Australia.

As I drove onto the grounds of the Catholic monastery where the Forge intensive was being held, I already felt out of my comfort zone. Dressed in my sports clothes—Michael Jordan shoes and a Jumpman hoodie—I walked past a room with a bunch of alternative-looking bikers and young people with dreadlocks. I figured it was an Alcoholics Anonymous recovery meeting. One of the bikers asked me who I was looking for, and I said, "Forge."

I had found them, he said.

I felt completely out of it. I felt like I stood out like a sore thumb. Their language, stories and contexts were all so different from where I had come from.

My imagination was more than expanded at Forge. God blew it completely up. On about the third day of this live-in intensive, I went back to my room, kneeled beside my bed and wept. I realized how much of a consumer Christian I had become. I felt like a heartless, selfish Christian compared to Ash Barker and Mick Duncan, who had described how they lived among the poor and learned from them, loving them like Jesus and sacrificing personal comforts, money and status for the sake of those they were sent to. I realized I had forgotten where I was raised—in one of the poorest suburbs in the state. I felt the conviction of the Holy Spirit.

The "sentness" they talked about was overwhelmingly convicting. For years I had not had the kind of passion and perseverance these people had. They were not the most polished or professional speakers I had ever heard. In a lot of cases they were single students or young moms who shared a passion for mission. But they were sold-out Christ followers who challenged my views about the church and the world.

It seemed that it did not matter if you were ordained or not, which denomination you came from (except if you were into prosperity theology) or the size of the thing you ran or were a part of. It was your story of sentness that people were interested in.

I became a sponge. I embraced the differences in language and context. I looked for the biblical principles that I could apply in Melbourne. Even though a lot of the stories at this intensive were around the urban poor, the people of Forge embraced me and my efforts planting a church among young people in the suburbs. I had found my tribe.

Alan Hirsch, one of the founders of Forge, took me aside. What had been missing from the Forge community, he said, was people whose passion was fueled by the fire of the Holy Spirit. Charismatic Christians tended to be less cynical and critical than many Christians; he saw our strengths as our faith in God to do and act and our desire to be led by the Spirit. Alan had found faith in the denomination I had grown up in; he told me that if my denominational tribe "got it," we would run with it with great effectiveness and fruitfulness.

Forge lit the fires of missional dreaming in me, and it gave me permission to do anything for God. It gave me a whole new community of cheerleaders and sojourners. Whenever I went to a Forge event, I was challenged again to think in new and fresh ways in regard to mission and ministry. Forge catapulted our family into ministry with the poor and shaped the very DNA of The Junction.

Forge also introduced me to inspiring mission-shaped leaders in Baptist, Churches of Christ, Salvation Army, Brethren, Seventh-day Adventist, Anglican, Vineyard, Oz Reach, Lutheran and other churches. As I began to interact with these new worlds, I found my learning and experience beginning to grow. God was increasing my missional imagination.

I graduated from Forge and volunteered there the year after. Just being around the team made me feel smarter, although they all read far more widely than I did, and I felt they were often more theologically intellectual than me—especially Alan, who intrigued me, and Mike Frost, who preached about Jesus from the Gospels and inspired me to change the world. I found my role in serving with practical details and helping people feel welcome. When a one-day-per-week administration job came up at Forge, I applied so I could stick close to the missionary thinkers and practitioners who network around Forge.

Meanwhile, we had opened our first Junction gathering in the front bar of the local pub. We all volunteered for a child-welfare agency, and we committed to eat, laugh, learn and love together as a missional community on a journey. We focused on mission, set our core values and DNA, and let the rest of our activity flow as needed. The team breathed with life and the excitement of new beginnings; we felt like pioneers in a new land, trying to be Jesus to a foreign people.

The meal became central to our gatherings, and our home and the local pub became sacred spaces for worship, teaching, prayer and celebration. I am so grateful for those first years. We had little idea what we were doing. But we knew we could do anything we felt led to do, as long as it fit into our culture and Scripture. We saw ourselves as modern-day translators of the gospel to a people group that had not heard it before.

We gave ourselves permission to experiment and try new things. There was plenty we did wrong and would do differently now, but I am forever grateful for all I learned about sentness from sharing life with my community at The Junction, and I will never forget rubbing shoulders with the crew at Forge Australia. These innovative missionaries blazed a trail for mission in the West before it was trendy.

Two Wings of the Same Bird

I (Darren) had been interested in global mission since high school. Back then, Keith Green sang "Jesus Commands Us to Go" and said that, with the Great Commission and the great needs overseas, it should be the exception if we stayed home. I resonated with Paul, who said, "My ambition has always been to preach the Good News where the name of Christ has never been heard, rather than where a church has already been started by someone else" (Romans 15:20). I read *Perspectives on the World Christian Movement*, which gave me insights into cutting-edge strategy in frontier missions.[3] While high school friends talked to career counselors, I wrote to mission agencies. I trained in education and Asian studies at university, met and married Jenni at Bible college, applied to our Baptist mission agency, enjoyed pastoral ministry in three churches, was ordained as a Baptist pastor and went to Indonesia.

We learned valuable lessons about mission during culture and language learning for Indonesia. Although our visas were as students and we were to be considered business entrepreneurs working on microenterprise development in ecotourism, we saw ourselves as missionaries. We were there to learn about our adopted people and to communicate the gospel in culturally appropriate ways.

For family and health reasons, we returned home to Australia. That was a vocational crisis for us, but it was also a vocational emergence: since we could not be missionaries in Indonesia, how could we instead be missionaries in our own local cultural context? What would it mean to apply the same missionary principles here at home: going as a learner, immersing ourselves in a local neighborhood, adopting community development principles, communicating the gospel in contextually appropriate ways and fostering church forms that are accessible to local people? What does sentness mean when we stay?

Missiologist Lesslie Newbigin shaped my realization that sentness applies to life at home as well as life on the mission field. Newbigin began his missionary career in India, where he stayed for three decades. When he returned to England, he looked at his home country with the same perspective he had used in India. He realized that England had itself become a huge unreached mission field. Late-modern Western culture, he determined, was post-Christian, pagan—"the most challenging missionary frontier of our time."[4] In "retirement," Newbigin served as a local pastor and urged other pastors to see themselves as missionary pastors, suggesting that "the only answer, the only hermeneutic of the gospel, is a congregation of men and women who believe it and live by it."[5]

I had loved being a pastor, so when we came home from Indonesia I reengaged with local church ministry. My first role for a year was as a pastoral change agent, helping two churches merge. After that we were called to Aberfeldie in Melbourne's inner-Western suburbs. Aberfeldie had a heritage of community engagement and local witness, and it involved some terrific people who were eager and open to fresh, mission-shaped leadership. But the church had been in decline for a decade and had recently experienced a conflict. It needed leadership that I admit now I was not equipped to give. We are thankful for some wonderful expressions of God's grace in individual lives over our three years there. But I did not manage to turn the congregation around or initiate much ongoing missional engagement. I had burning questions about how to revitalize and refocus local churches for mission, when and how to plant new congregations, and how to train missional leaders. I brought these questions to Forge; intrigued by Alan Hirsch's and Mike Frost's writing, I wanted to research case studies of emerging missional churches and see what I could learn from them. I also wanted to observe what missional churches still needed to learn.

Kim asked me to help Forge engage with theological colleges. Often it felt like the teaching content we prepared was peripheral to the stories of practitioners having a go at all sorts of innovative experiments. At the same time, I was curious to explore the actual innovation and mission in a few recently started churches in Melbourne, compared against the framework established by Frost and Hirsch's *The Shaping of Things to Come*. You will read about some of my Melbourne case studies, as well as stories from Kim and from around America and the world, in coming chapters. It is exciting to see and be a part of a fresh wave of sentness that God is releasing.[6]

SHIFT TO SENTNESS

How do we recapture a missional imagination? What is God doing that we can join in on? What is God calling us to and sometimes out of? Where and how are people realizing and living out their sentness?

Someone has said that the ideal missionary has the heart of an evangelist and the mind of a scholar. We are eager to cultivate both. As pastors and as missionary trainers, we love bringing missional leaders and thinkers, speakers and writers into conversation with local practitioners to learn from one another. We have appreciated learning from smart people, but we do not expect everyone to become a professor. In fact, educational expectations (and aspirations) can sometimes distract people from grassroots mission; meanwhile, some of the best missionaries we know have no formal education in theology.

We love to celebrate and learn from both Christian tradition and the best of contemporary experiments. We are committed and sold out to a radical missiology, but our roots remain in orthodox theology.[7] We stand in a Christian evangelical tradition that is boldly confident in Jesus and the Bible, and in the power of the gospel to transform people and communities.[8] And we honor the long history of writers, thinkers and theologians who have contributed to this conversation.

From Karl Barth, Lesslie Newbigin and David Bosch to Darrell Guder, Alan Roxburgh and others in the Gospel and Our Culture Network, there are many missional thinkers to whom we owe a debt of gratitude. Urban mission, radical discipleship, systems theory, organizational theory, alternative worship, house churches, emerging churches, Emergent, Pentecostalism and the New Monasticism are all movements and conversations we have learned from.[9] There is one central element we always gravitate back to, however: what is it to be sent?

This is the main thing we have learned from our involvement with Forge Mission Training Network—the importance of framing all we do with being missional. As Hirsch has taught us, new forms of church best emerge when they start by being missional.[10] Churches need to contextualize their worship and communication, ask themselves how they can be more seeker-sensitive, do what it takes to grow in numbers and advocate for social justice. But these aims should serve the church's primary focus, which is ultimately the mission of God.[11]

Sentness is not only the proper organizing principle for our churches; it's also the foundation for our individual discipleship. Formation is not for any other purpose than for mission. If we are going to connect with those who currently have so little connection with the church, first our imaginations must be grabbed by *why* we would reach them in the first place.

LIVING APE SOCIETY

Recently I (Kim) got to be a part of one of the largest missions conferences in North America, InterVarsity's Urbana 2012 conference. Some twenty thousand young people came together to worship from across the world. As a guest of InterVarsity/USA, I got to meet some of their incredible leaders, including Beau Crosetto. Beau has started a group called Release the APE to encourage those with apostolic, prophetic and evangelism gifts (APE = Apostles, Prophets, Evangelists) to speak into the mission of the church and to reproduce themselves. I sat in a gathering of about two dozen young leaders that Beau had convened at eleven at night. I am nearly forty, and I was the oldest person there by far. Most were in their early twenties. Beau encouraged them to share their stories, hopes and dreams. We laid hands on groups of them, praying for those who felt they needed to respond more deeply to God's calling.

I had planned to sit and observe and say nothing, but it wasn't too long before I was called on to encourage and equip some of these amazing leaders. As they poured out of the room at one in the morning, many asked me for books to read and resources to devour. Their hunger is typical of many emerging leaders longing to see a shift from consumer Christianity to sentness.

A similar shift is in view in the 1989 film *Dead Poets Society*. Prep-school English professor John Keating engages his students in quite unorthodox prep-school behavior: he takes them out of their classroom, inspires them to tear boring parts out of their textbook, and inspires them to revive the school's old Dead Poets Society, a secret gathering of students reading poetry in a cave. In one class he invites them to stand up on their desks to see the world from a different perspective. Keating encourages the students to "seize the day" (*carpe diem*) and to realize the potential they have.

We need to help emerging leaders dream again about mission in the West. Forge functions like that—we gather living prophets and apostles and evangelists, along with pastors and teachers, to share their stories and learn from one another. It's a living APE society, spurring Christians to allow apostolic, prophetic and evangelistic ministry to flourish in the church and, by extension, in the world.

The challenges of contemporary Western society demand that our paradigms for mission change. But paradigm changes are not easy and never without cost. Sadly, many people are giving up on church in the process. Forge offers a theological framework, a network and formation for staying with the church and drawing the church to what it should be. Mike Frost says Forge functions for many like a peg or anchor in the ground for what church is meant to be.

We wanted to call this book *Practicing the Missionary Position and Loving It.* Some thought it too rude or crude, but for us it reflects a lost truth: the basic position the church needs to assume in the world is that of a missionary. To shift our understanding beyond consumerism and to grow a tribe of missionaries who understand their sentness, we need to practice six missional postures:

- sent people, understanding that God has a mission and that mission has a church

- submerged ministry, following Jesus and moving among places and people

- shalom spirituality, seeking restoration for individuals, communities and all things

- safe places, for people from diverse backgrounds to find faith and community

- sharing life, forming teams around a common vision and strength of relationships

- standing in the gap, empowering pioneering leaders and missional experiments

The chapters in this book will unpack each of these missional postures. Taken together, the chapters constitute the genius of sentness, which breaks the bonds of consumer Christianity and prepares us for the mission of God.

Wherever you are and wherever you are sent, we hope you will be equipped, coached and convinced that God has gone ahead of you, has brought you there and is working with you to foster the kingdom of God. Whether your mission is across the street or on the other side of the world, there is no difference in our commitment or passion for you to have the vision and skills you need for cooperating with God in sentness.

If you are engaged in missional experiments of sentness or trying something new as a result of reading this book, we would love to hear from you. Please contact us through our website:

www.sentnessbook.com

1

BEYOND CONSUMERISM

Give us each day the food we need,
and forgive us our sins,
as we forgive those who sin against us.
And don't let us yield to temptation.

Jesus (Luke 11:3-4)

Pastors of America have metamorphosed into a company
of shopkeepers, and the shops they keep are churches.

Eugene Peterson

JAKE SULLY IS PARALYZED—in his world. But in another world, his body is bigger and stronger.

We are talking about the lead character of James Cameron's 2009 movie *Avatar*.[1] In the colorful and larger-than-life Na'vi environment, Jake meets the beautiful Neytiri, the warrior princess who initiates him into Na'vi culture. Together they face deadly struggles and lay their lives on the line. But the story goes beyond romance.

Part of the courageous adventure for Jake, as he bonds with the Na'vi, is seeing a vision for a better world and joining them in their struggle against environmental rape and land theft.

Some humans see the Na'vi world only with consumerist and materialist eyes. They see only what they can sell and what they can get out of it for themselves. They see the Na'vi people fighting for their survival and taking a stand to defend their culture and environment, but they ignore the injustice in their desire to get rich.

Jake himself is tempted to overlook the Na'vis' pain and side with the oppressors. As incentive, he is promised a special operation to get the use of his legs back. He considers not staying with his adopted people and returning to his own world and its material rewards. But he comes to understand that his sentness gives him a special responsibility. The shift in the story comes as Jake and a handful of sympathetic friends stand in solidarity with the Na'vi in their struggle.

Jake's adventure has an incarnational and missional undertone. Jake is Christlike in taking on Na'vi flesh and becoming one of them. He moves into their neighborhood and dwells among them, and he fights against that which threatens to steal, kill and destroy (see John 1:14; 10:10). He leads the struggle for their lives and their culture, drawing together Na'vi from different tribes. His struggle is even to the point of death in his old body, and he comes back to life in his new body, and he stays then in the context in which he has been sent (see Philippians 2:5-11).

WHO'S THE ADDICT?

Avatar is an indictment of our consumerist world, which so often puts things before people and economic progress over environmental concerns. Since the Industrial Revolution and the onset of mass production and capitalism, our industries and businesses have sought to produce more and sell more. Workers moved from towns and villages into cities to be the necessary labor force. Marketing developed to tell people about the products they could buy to meet their needs. Then the whole advertising industry overdeveloped to tell people what their needs should be so they would buy more and more.

There is, as a result, pressure to consume whether we really need things or not, for the sake of our appearance, our identity. Isn't it disgusting that an advertisement says, "Everyone deserves a luxury car at least once in their lifetime," when the lifetimes of twenty thousand children will end today because of starvation and preventable disease? Our economy and world system is failing to operate in a sustainable way as the environment and global warming show the costs of our conspicuous consumption. And building our identity based on the things we own and consume destroys our souls.

In Melbourne, we often took Forge students to visit Urban Seed, a mission based in Collins Street Baptist Church. Urban Seed was a partner, with a woman named Sally Quinn, in launching the nonprofit social enterprise Green Collect,[2] which offers a range of environmental services to businesses and hospitality venues. Green Collect provides training and work to disadvantaged people, people who have had barriers to employment. Green Collect also has engaged in waste collection and recycling, starting with bottle corks and later expanding to mobile phones and toner cartridges. Now they offer waste audits to local businesses, challenging the throwaway mentality of a consumerist society, which is willing to discard products and even people without caring about the implications.

This creative response by Urban Seed to the problems of their community runs counter to the consumerist mentality on display on Collins Street. If we define *religion* as what gives people identity, belonging and purpose, then consumerism is the dominant religious alternative to Christianity in Western countries.

Consumerism drives much of society. Everyone consumes, of course. It's how we are made; we consume to survive. Consuming is okay. But consumption can expand from something basic to life to something that defines life. We get our identity from collecting possessions and experiences. Malls are our cathedrals. For many, shopping is the preferred means of therapy and of feeling good. The back door of Urban Seed's offices opens onto "Baptist Lane," which was a major hub for heroin users, with a high incidence of overdoses and ambulance calls. The front door of Urban Seed, meanwhile, opens onto Collins Street between Town Hall and State Parliament, one of the most prestigious shopping streets in Melbourne. The church has recently opened the Verandah Cafe to express welcome and hospitality to people passing by on the street. The church is at the "Paris" end, where you can buy expensive clothing, accessories and jewelry. Every year, Urban Seed takes more than ten thousand students on city tours out of the front and back doors of the church. And then they ask, "Where are the addicts?"

As pervasive as consumerism has become, it's maybe not surprising that it's had an impact on contemporary Christianity. Individual Christians "shop around" for a local church that they think will best suit their needs. Churches identify the particular needs of local people and seek to show how the church addresses those needs. Pastors feel pressured to become providers of religious goods and services—a decidedly consumer-driven approach to ministry—rather than helping their people become more focused on the mission of God in the world. Some people think Islam and atheism are the biggest challenges to Christian faith. But we maintain that consumerism is far more challenging and pervasive. And it influences not just people outside the church but also those of us in the church, affecting our whole approach to what we believe and practice.

BEYOND CHURCH SHOPPING

When we get to heaven, can you imagine the discussion with Christians who were persecuted in their times and regions, asking us what was the hardest thing for us? What would their response be if we were to say, "When the church parking lot is full" or "When the singing takes too long"? They would look at us in disbelief and confusion. In any other time in history, can you imagine Christians not going to church because the parking lot was full or because the singing went too long?

Only in the Western world do you hear the phrase "church shopping." American Christians go to church on average 1.4 times a month; we are going less and getting busier. We say we want community and to belong to something bigger than ourselves, yet we change church communities like we change gym memberships. Obviously there are sometimes legitimate reasons to move on. Sometimes God calls us and sends us to new places. However, there is an increasing amount of choice based on consumption rather than calling or commitment to community.

In response to church shopping, churches feel pressure to keep that hour of worship, 1.4 times a month, nonconfrontational. People show up and stare at the back of someone else's head, never knowing what is happening in that person's life. We come to get rather than to give to one another or to the world.

We have been privileged to serve as pastors while also having training roles for most of the previous fifteen years. We have felt the pressure through most of those years, if not most weeks, to manage our churches to deliver religious goods and services. People expect it. The system is designed for it. And meeting those expectations makes us feel good and needed. But it is not church as God designed it to be.

As Christians, we need what Australian poet Michael Leunig cleverly calls an "understandogram": we need to examine our culture and society and understand what lies underneath our beliefs and behavior. Consumer church does not require enough from its members. It can't because, schooled by a consumerist society, people look for a church as a place to go to meet their needs, rather than a base to be sent from to serve their community. We consider what we got out of the church service, and we go home feeling well fed or not. Thus church turns into a mall for consuming religious goods and services, rather than an equipping station to send us into our world.

Those not willing to deal with their issues within the confines of a trusting community tend not to stay in one church for long. If pressure to contribute and serve is applied, people transfer to where there is less pressure, carrying with them their unresolved issues. We need others to speak into our problems with conviction and truth.

Who created church consumerism? We contend that all of us did. Well, maybe you could blame the devil, but we are the propagators of the virus. And the world outside the church sees the false community propagated there by consumerism, the hypocrisy and judgment, and wants little to do with it.

But the good news is, there is more to church than that.

We are not talking about a new style of church or a different program. We have seen some "organic house churches," which claim to be more missional than their more traditionally organized church neighbors, define themselves by what they are against—like buildings and Sunday services. Some of them are, ironically, more consumerist than many of the large churches they criticize. Meanwhile, we have visited more traditionally structured churches that in the life rhythms of their members and the culture of their community remind us of Jesus. So we're not calling for new programs, nor are we rejecting traditional forms of church. We are, rather, grappling with the foundational images competing for the minds of Christians today. Consumerism is a dominant temptation, not just in terms of how we live in the world but also of how we function as church.

WHAT HAPPENS WHEN PEOPLE LOSE THEIR SENTNESS?

You can tell when people have not embraced their sentness. They talk about the church in the third person. They talk about it as an entity out there to be criticized and consumed. They do not see church as God intended: a gathering of the called ones, the set apart ones.

People who have lost their sentness expect their church to deliver on its promises to meet their needs, to care for them, to make them feel good. Pastors who have lost their sentness see their primary responsibilities as organizing services and meeting the needs of the people who are paying the bills. People who have lost their sentness gauge the success of their pastors according to metrics related to sales: more customers, more money and, ideally, a more fancy showroom. In other words, we measure church success by buildings, butts on seats and bucks in the offering.

Pastor Eugene Peterson writes about this epidemic in the Western church:

> Pastors of America . . . are preoccupied with shopkeeper's concerns—how to keep the customers happy, how to lure customers away from competitors down the street, how to package the goods so that customers will lay out more money. Some of them are very good shopkeepers. They attract a lot of customers, pull in great sums of money, and develop splendid reputations. Yet, it is still shopkeeping; religious shopkeeping to be sure, but shopkeeping all the same. The marketing strategies of the fast-food franchise occupy the waking minds of these entrepreneurs; while asleep they dream of the kind of successes that will get the attention of journalists.[3]

It is this kind of bland, entertainment-based church life that is turning people off from Christianity.

Churches everywhere are asking how to create systems for discipleship. And the larger the church, the more the system needs to be simple and reproducible. We have interacted with some of the fastest-growing churches in America, which are brilliant at rolling out initiatives or systems that influence the entire church. These churches have a lot to teach us. However, we think discipleship is more about creating a culture than about creating a system. When we get the culture right—when we tap into the missional DNA of the body of Christ—people become better disciples.

CONSUMING AND PRODUCING

One way we encourage Christians to move beyond consumerism is by balancing consumption with production. It is appropriate to consume, but we need to integrate consuming with producing so that we are not preoccupied by the drive to consume.

The slow food movement is a protest against the utilitarian approach that produces and eats standardized, tasteless food as efficiently and quickly as possible—whether convenient fast food eaten on the run or frozen dinners eaten without conversation in front of the television. Slow food brings production and consumption as close together as possible, so we don't have to transport foods from one side of the country to another, with all the related environmental costs and the reduction in food's health value that comes from freezing and so on. It also encourages us to eat slowly and healthily.

Bloggers Chris Smith and John Pattison have developed an understanding of church inspired by the slow food movement. Their "slow church" encourages Christians to protest against the drivenness of speed and efficiency and to reconnect locally where God plants us. It encourages attentiveness to sustainable ecology, economics, ethics and local community development, which starts with slowing down and being faithfully present and attentive to what God is doing locally.[4]

Urban Seed has been similarly inspired by the slow food

movement.[5] In the center of Melbourne, their Credo Café invites dozens of people around the table for midweek lunchtimes. It is not a soup kitchen feeding hundreds of people, but a community meal, where people from diverse socioeconomic backgrounds—from people who are homeless and struggling with addictions to corporate employees working in nearby office buildings—produce and eat a meal together.

Urban Seed's worship is similarly inspired by the slow food movement—not by singing slower songs but by integrating worship with local rhythms and using local resources and icons. New Zealand alternative worship curator Mark Pierson helped Credo Café to include a breadth of people's backgrounds, stages of faith, traditions and learning styles in the worship that grew out of their community meals. Instead of seeking first to meet people's spiritual needs, Urban Seed invites people to contribute to all aspects of a gathering—from invitation through music and engagement with the Bible to prayers for the world and sending out. The resulting culture and liturgy leads to more thoughtful consumption as well as increasing production among the gathered worshipers.

Participation is not a new idea. Paul's teaching on charismatic worship celebrates the contribution of all God's people: "When you meet together, one will sing, another will teach, another will tell some special revelation God has given, one will speak in tongues, and another will interpret what is said" (1 Corinthians 14:26). God invites people to taste and experience his goodness (Psalm 34:8). Jesus invites all sorts of people to sit around his table and share his hospitality and his body and blood as represented in the Lord's Supper (Luke 22:14-20).

There is also a sense that God invites us to consume—to consume and experience the fullness and life of God's very self. And God provides all sorts of good things in the world for us to enjoy and benefit from. God placed people in the garden of Eden with all the fruit and food they needed (Genesis 2:4-16). When God delivered Israel from Egypt, he provided manna and quail in the desert (Exodus 16:1-18).

But those stories also show us where people get greedy. The Israelites disobeyed God's instruction to collect only enough manna for each day; they tried to store up extra manna to put aside for another day (Exodus 16:19-20). Adam and Eve were not content with a lavish spread of food in the garden but stretched also for the forbidden fruit (Genesis 2:17–3:6). Early church disciples enjoyed the Lord's Supper, but some rich believers hogged the food for themselves and ignored the needs of their poorer sisters and brothers (1 Corinthians 11:17-34). And after the feeding of the five thousand, when the teaching got difficult and things arose to complain about, many disciples deserted Jesus (John 6:60-71).

One Sunday morning a mom was cooking pancakes for her two sons. You might be surprised to hear that Eddie and Murray started to fight over who could eat the first pancake. Mom saw the opportunity for a moral lesson. "Boys, boys," she said, "don't argue—if Jesus was here he'd say, 'Let my brother have the first pancake.'" Mom was pleased when Murray's eyes grew large with understanding. He turned to his younger brother and said, "Eddie, you be Jesus."

Left to our own natural tendencies, we choose religious paths that best suit us and ways of following Jesus that are most satisfying for us. But that path falls far short of the discipleship put forward in the Bible. And it does not foster an outward-looking, world-embracing, missional church. It turns Jesus into a cosmic butler who is there to serve us or a therapist to make us feel better or a career coach to help us get ahead or an image consultant to make us look successful. The habit of following Jesus in ways that suit us needs to be unlearned.

WHAT DOES IT MEAN TO BE A SENT PEOPLE?

There is an alternative to consumer church: a church of *sent people*. Sent people understand that just as God sent his Son into the world, Jesus sends us to continue his work and share his life. Sent people realize that their reason for existence is not to consume but to serve. When we understand our sentness, we see our families and our neighborhoods, our workplaces and our communities with fresh eyes. We submerge ourselves in our communities, embrace a spirituality of the everyday sort, foster safe places and stand in the gap for others.

Solace is a congregation started by Olivia Maclean that grew out of St. Hilary's Anglican Church in Melbourne.[6] A group of people there wanted to move on from worshiping with pews and prayer books to exploring more creative and participatory worship for all ages and all stages of faith. Solace has since branched off from St. Hilary's and has moved several times, and they continue to experiment with interactive and participatory worship. But their main focus is to be a network for people to empower their everyday spirituality and mission.

With a vision to "revitalize through Christian spirituality," Solace views itself as "a network that helps people enjoy authentic, Jesus-centered, spirituality in their everyday lives."[7] They help people reflect on their passions and dreams, and they celebrate stories of people being better neighbors, friends, advocates, businesspeople, teachers, nurses and environmental workers. They express their reason for existence in their mission statement: "To Enable a People to Thrive as Followers of Jesus, Celebrating and Re-making Their Everyday World." Empowering people to celebrate life and to develop a vision for making the world a better place—a place more in line with God's dream for the world—is central to the Solace ethos.

Solace sees the "gathered church" in worship and meetings as the training ground for people's real work of ministry as they "scatter" throughout the week. Leaders encourage participation in gatherings

to the extent that it is life giving; they discourage attending everything so that life doesn't get too busy to be authentically spiritual.
Pastors and staff see their work as a "back office" role to support
what they believe is the real work of ministry in the sentness of their
members. Solace regularly celebrates everyday stories of vocation:
friendships, tree planting, artistic expression, letter writing, nursing
and whatever work or community involvement people engage in.

Stuart Davey has collected stories, artwork and exercises from
Solace for the book *Remaking*, to illustrate the group's seven Jesus-
centered ways—described on their website as Contemplation,
Everyday, Word, Spirit, Justice, Relating and Wholeness. *Remaking*
celebrates God working not just *in* church but *beyond* it. It envi-
sions Christ's body, the church, filling everything (Ephesians 1:23)
and remaking the world. Solace's agenda is thus helping members
live out Jesus' ways wherever they are sent: "all the places you live,
visit, work in, belong to and all the people around you."[8]

Solace has recognized that the very essence of God is mission,
which guides God's redemptive purposes. They often discuss what
they discern God is doing in their community and how they might
join in. They view God as the initiator and themselves as apprentices to and partners with God. They understand that just as God
sent Jesus into the world, God sends them to incarnate his presence
and remake their world in line with God's dream.

Solace resists operating as a vendor of religious goods and services and seeks instead to establish a cooperative network of like-
minded ministers and a people sent on mission.[9] They do not strive
to meet everyone's felt needs with church programs. Rather, if
leaders see a need, they encourage members to try to create something that fills it and to invite others to join.

Solace has been moving beyond consumerism since they started
with the intention of equipping people for mission rather than just
entertaining them in church. And yet they are intentional and cre-

ative with alternative expressions of worship and encourage high participation. Their gatherings are informed by adult learning principles, include multisensory worship and are typically informal and authentic, with lots of discussion, questioning and interaction. Olivia sees worship gatherings as like a game of Hacky Sack: anyone can start or add to a conversation, people learn as they contribute, and a game is not successful until everyone participates.

The people of Solace see the "Seven Ways" not just as a means for spiritual formation but as an entry point for people into Christianity. Realizing we live in a world that is consumerist but also spiritually hungry, they seek to entice people to faith in Jesus through inviting them to foster a spiritual side of their lives. It has also been important for Solace to guide people beyond the merely personal and individualized approach to faith that is typical of consumerism. They worship a God who is relevant to all aspects of life and who invites people to integrate their interests, service and work with their vocation. People of Solace express their allegiance to a God who is interested in all spheres, rather than longing for individual tribal deities who will bless particular spheres based on individual interests. They point to a faith that can address the biggest issues in our world: "To believe in a God who will protect you from car accidents and find you car parks," they contend, "sounds more like relying on fate rather than developing a spirituality which supplies meaning and hope."[10]

Solace demonstrates that spirituality is at its best when it helps us embrace our sentness. Such spirituality invites us to move beyond the self-interested allure of consumerism and foster instead the kingdom of God wherever we are sent.

MEGACHURCHES AND MOVEMENTS

It is not just small, new or emerging groups like Solace or Urban Seed that are moving beyond consumerism to sentness. There is a movement of churches of all shapes and sizes grappling with these issues—including megachurches.

Megachurches can be machines, albeit very well-oiled ones. Some of them are like Hollywood production companies: they produce amazing shows and attract big audiences. Some of their pastors are like rock stars, with fans and an entourage, a fully stocked green room and a contract rider to match. They write best-sellers and command large crowds. To be fair, they usually are incredibly gifted and make big sacrifices, but the temptation to have an ego to match the size of their organization, and to strive for bigger buildings and budgets simply for the sake of it, is huge.

While some churches are stuck thinking about their next event and how to fill their seats, however, some megachurch leaders are developing a missional movement. Dave Ferguson of Community Christian Church in Naperville, Illinois, and Brian Bloye of Westridge Church Atlanta, for example, both planted the churches they lead, and they have been faithful in leading those churches over two decades each. But they also both made decisions not just to get bigger but to plant more churches. This has resulted in two significant church-planting networks: the New Thing Network, born out of Community Christian, which plants a new church every eleven days; and the Launch Network, born out of Westridge, which partners with other churches to equip planters to lead strongly. Both pastors have decided that the churches they lead will send rather than just consume.

These leaders' influence and capacity means they grow things large and fast. However, the thing we admire most about them is their heart to see cities and communities restored—their own and beyond. It is inspiring to see the way they are encouraging young women and men to discover and embrace their sentness.

Ferguson and Bloye help lead a gathering of megachurch and multisite leaders in America who are experimenting with what it means to become genuine missional movements. Both have authored books and have influence across the church world. Yet they are both lifelong learners. With a group of peers they were part of the original Future Travelers—basically peer clusters of ten to twelve churches seeking to implement organic missional principles alongside existing megachurch models of growth. I (Kim) have been privileged to participate and to help Alan Hirsch host and lead some of the gatherings of these leaders.

Part of the genius of Future Travelers is that they seek to make the most of the contribution of strong mission-resourcing churches and catalyze the creativity of missional experiments, while they are also committed to learning from the best "attractional" models operating within the parameters of a consumer culture. These churches encourage each other in continuing to reproduce on a macro scale (new churches and campuses) but also increasingly on a micro scale (mobilizing every believer for mission in everyday life and organic church planting).[11]

We get the sense that Future Travelers want to create a culture that gives permission for local mission experiments at all levels. They are creating a new language that affirms a new generation of missionaries and helps Christians move beyond consumerism. These megachurches still have large services with buildings, but their posture is one of sentness. Ferguson, for example, once shut down all church services at twelve campuses so the whole Community Christian community could go out and serve their city. He drives a beat-up 1982 Honda, sits in an open office and receives a modest salary (by megachurch standards). Similarly, Bloye chairs the group Engage Atlanta; every month I (Kim) watch him pray for hours for the needs of those in his church by name. Both men take a personal and corporate stand against consumerism and are personally and corporately embracing their sentness.

It is easy, in a consumerist age, to judge quickly and critique loudly. But we have been learning to celebrate mission and sentness where we see it, and to learn what we can from one another across all different styles of church. I (Kim) recently met Rick Warren, pastor of the massive Saddleback Community Church—a frequent target of "missional" purists. In a small, closed meeting of Forge America, he sat and took notes, and at the end of the day he offered some great advice on movements. In Forge, we call people like Ferguson, Bloye and Warren unleaders;[12] it is all about the posture.

SIGNS OF A WELL-SENT PEOPLE

Are you tired of looking for a church to meet all your needs? Do you want to stop *going* to church and instead *be* the church? If so, you will need to be brave and sacrificial. You will have to put your own preferences and likes aside. You will have to fight the tide of popular culture wooing you to be like the crowd and consume.

It is tempting to read and get excited about the mission of God and the opportunity to change to a paradigm of sentness, and then to go back to church business as usual. We are conditioned to do this by a consumer culture, to play with new ideas and see how they benefit us. But we will advance the kingdom of God not through just thinking new ideas and talking about innovative approaches to church, but by demonstrating their reality. People who are caught up in consumer church are good people, but they have no idea they are killing the church.

You have the responsibility to shift—yourself and your faith community—from a consumer mindset to a posture of sentness. The question is, do you have the courage? Maybe you can keep drawing customers and giving out goods and services. But ultimately customers leave for a better product.

Don't get us wrong. We are all for being generous in our gatherings. We can't stand cruddy coffee. With our wives, Maria and Jenni, we have always enjoyed hospitable living with what we have.

Of course we can be attractive in how we do church as we emphasize the importance of sentness. But we kill sentness when we put *all* our resources and time into the Sunday show—elevating our gatherings and making them more important than equipping the whole church to live on mission. We are convinced that when mission is the organizing principle of the church, we gather and grow and pray in the middle of that process.

Sentness is within your reach. You can do it. It starts with stopping the criticizing and simply embracing your sentness.

Sentness is not, however, just about finding ourselves in a particular place and being content that God has sent us there. It also involves submerging ourselves among the places and people God has sent us to, fostering shalom spirituality for them and cultivating safe places for people of diverse backgrounds to explore the meaning of faith.

Sentness also means sharing life with the teams and tribes God sends us with and standing in the gap to empower others and their dreams for mission. As we are sent, rather than looking for the next best thing that suits our needs, we will start new things to serve others. These are the signs of a well-sent people.

2

SENT PEOPLE

Peace be with you.
As the Father has sent me, so I am sending you.

JESUS (JOHN 20:21)

The missional-incarnational church will make Christian teaching
attractive by living it under the very noses of those
who have not yet embraced it.

MICHAEL FROST AND ALAN HIRSCH

IT NEVER CEASES TO AMAZE US how God is a God of surprises. God calls and draws and sends people to fulfill his purposes in amazing ways. We pray God will never cease to surprise you. We pray you will be open to the surprising presence and voice of Jesus. We pray for the children in your church and for those who are older, those who are new to church and faith and those who have been around for years—that you would be aware of Jesus' presence and freshly hear his voice.

Jesus was full of surprises. He turned the tables on people's expectations. At one stage he turned the tables literally on people's religious activity. His death was undeserved but a natural consequence of his life and teaching; he surprised the world by his sacrifice, demonstrating his love to the point of death and defeating evil so thoroughly. In his mind-blowing resurrection, he surpassed all human expectations. Jesus is surprising. And we love that about him.

Can you imagine Jesus appearing to his disciples after his resurrection? The miracle of it is mind blowing. But the grace Jesus showed the disciples and the way he invited them to follow him in being sent into the world and to carry on his work is also mind blowing. The disciples were thrown by the circumstances. Critical and politically oriented people surrounded them. They were scared, perhaps of following Jesus and dying as well. But then Jesus was there, and his words were so welcome.

These were the disciples who had run away and denied him. They had ignored or forgotten his words of hope (or had them scared out of them). They hid behind a locked door. They gathered without confidence or hope or direction. And Jesus came to them, and he restored their hope. He surprised them with beautiful words of grace and peace, forgiveness and commissioning: "Peace be with you. As the Father has sent me, so am I sending you" (John 20:21).

Those were probably not the words the disciples were expecting. Jesus came with a nonanxious presence. Sometimes that is the best gift a leader can give to a group. Jesus came saying "Peace be with you" rather than "You idiots, why did you leave me holding the ball alone?" What a pleasant surprise. Jesus does that. And we love that about him.

"Peace be with you. As the Father has sent me, so I am sending you." Are those words that you can hear from Jesus? When we are disappointed with ourselves (or feel the disappointment of others), we need these words of grace from Jesus. When we are paralyzed by concerns, we are desperate for a surprising word of peace. When we expect too much of ourselves or drive ourselves to do more than we need to, these words can help us to slow down. Whether we are sitting comfortably behind closed doors or trying to figure out how or when to go beyond the walls of our church, we find encouragement in Jesus' words to the first disciples: "Peace be with you. As the Father has sent me, so I am sending you."

How long since you grasped these words from Jesus? Churches sometimes host "seeker" services as safe places where not-yet-believers can seek knowledge about God. Actually, the best seeker services are when we let God freshly seek and find *us*. Rediscovering and experiencing the sent and sending Jesus of the Gospels is essential to embracing our sentness. If we can see a fresh vision of who Jesus is for us and for the world, it transforms how we relate to the world.

World Vision worker Tim Dearborn believes that a lack of interest in mission is

> not caused by an absence of compassion or commitment, not by lack of information or exhortation. And lack of interest in mission is not remedied by more shocking statistics, more gruesome stories or more emotionally manipulative commands to obedience. It is best remedied by intensifying people's passion for Christ, so that the passions of his heart become the passions that propel our hearts.[1]

God had only one Son, and he sent him to us as a missionary. *In the same way, you are sent into your world.* You have the same mandate to foster the kingdom of God and to share what really is good news about Jesus. You won't die on a cross and be raised again to save the world. But you are sent as a representative or ambassador of Jesus, who did live, die and rise from the dead to transform the lives of people and nations. We are sent so that people who have not met the risen Lord might discover what he is really like, by seeing what he has done in our lives.

There is a story about how Jesus ascended from the Mount of Olives and was welcomed back by the angels with a big party. One said, "Lord, let's go now, and tell the world how you conquered the powers of darkness and death."

Jesus replied, "No, it's not going to be like that."

The angel asked, "What do you mean? This is the moment we've been waiting for."

"I have another plan."

"What other plan?"

Jesus looked at the disciples, disappearing like ants below them, and said, "They're going to do it. . . ."

"Them—do you trust them? What if they fail?"

"We have no other plan. It is their destiny, their responsibility, their commission to carry the message to people everywhere."[2]

It's exciting that God has a plan that includes us—in Chicago or Cleveland, Dallas or Detroit, Melbourne or Manchester or Mumbai—to do whatever it takes, however radical it is (within the ethical bounds of the gospel), to make Christ known.

Let our imaginations be captured afresh by Jesus and his words to us: "Peace be with you." Be assured by his peace and forgiveness. And, "as the Father has sent me, so I am sending you." Be assured of your call and commission as a missionary.

BREATHING GOD'S SPIRIT

Jesus did not stop there with this surprising display of grace to his disciples. He demonstrated that he understands our pain and hurt and doubt. He turned to Thomas, who had doubted his resurrection, and showed him the one thing he takes to heaven, the one reminder of his time on earth as a human being: his scars, his brokenness. The sins of all humankind are represented in this wounding of an immortal God and King. And even in this, Jesus was gracious: he did not rebuke Thomas for his doubts but simply stretched his hands out to him. We love that about Jesus.

Then Jesus faced all of them and breathed on them, saying, "Receive the Holy Spirit." Can you picture Jesus breathing on us, and as we inhale air from his lungs, we receive the same Spirit that filled and fueled him? This is not something we work for or get as a reward. It is not a one-time experience, but a process of being refilled and continually breathing the presence of Jesus and the Spirit.

As kids, my friends and I (Darren) would take a deep breath and hold it as we rode bicycles down a hill until we either gave up and took a breath or blacked out. We thought it was a real hoot watching each other crash. It was admittedly a stupid exercise, but how often do we try to rely on a breath of God's Spirit from a past event? To move beyond walls, we need to keep breathing in, continually relying on God's Spirit, so that we can move out with Spirit-inspired direction: words to say, compassion for the hurting, power for healing and faith in prayer. Jesus wants to tell dangerous stories in and through our lives, and his mission for us is as a *sent* people, filled with the Holy Spirit.

PORTRAIT OF A SENDING GOD

We do not live in the outskirts of Indonesia, the slums of Cambodia or the poorest villages of Africa. We are not in an apartment in Paris or Prague. But wherever we are, God sends us.

Being sent by Jesus is not about waiting for a future opportunity. It does not happen only when we hop on a plane. Our mission is often right in front of us in our neighborhood, workplace or city. If we are *sent* where we are, then we *stay* with it and discern how we can work with what God is doing around and in and through us. Don't wait for more money, a promotion, the right situation, the ideal job. Don't look for something that will win you a Nobel Prize.

Don't overthink it. The ultimate thing is hearing Jesus' words of peace to us and then letting him send us to share that peace with others. As Howard Snyder said,

> Church people think about how to get people into the church; kingdom people think about how to get the church into the world. Church people worry that the world might change the church; kingdom people work to see the church change the world.[3]

A missiologist who helped us to grasp that God is a sending God is South African David Bosch, who wrote the most significant book on missiology in the last century, *Transforming Mission*. In it he describes the six eras and paradigm shifts of mission history, from the apostolic era through to today's postmodern and ecumenical paradigm. His most helpful insight for embracing our sentness is how the church's missional basis is grounded in *missio Dei*—"the mission of God" or "the missionary God."

> Mission was understood as being derived from the very nature of God . . . Father, Son, and Holy Spirit sending the church into the world . . . a movement from God to the world; the church is viewed as an instrument for that mission. . . . There is a church because there is a mission, not vice versa.[4]

Missio Dei is dangerous for the consumer church's preconceptions about the world. It means *the church does not bear ultimate responsibility for mission*. The mission belongs to God.

Mission is all that God is doing in the world to bring the world back into line with his dream for it. The church's privilege is that God invites us to cooperate. God *sends* people to cooperate with what God wants to do in the world. *Missio Dei* is the basis of our sentness and the path beyond consumer Christianity.

The Gospel and Our Culture Network (GOCN) has been calling

the church in North America to find its identity in mission and let that influence the church's shape. The church in the West is marginalized from its prior roles and has often overaccommodated to modern culture. The book *Missional Church,* edited by Darrell Guder as a GOCN resource, suggests that the best response is not to reintroduce new methods or problem solving, but to clarify the church's identity and task. The church is not primarily a voluntary association, a chaplain to society or a vendor of religious goods and services. It is not intrinsically here to *sell.* Rather the church is an alternative community that witnesses by living differently. The church is a body characterized by *sentness.*[5]

CAN I BE SENT JUST A LITTLE?

Sentness is not just for missionaries to foreign lands. The shift is for all of us—students and workers, parents and kids, professionals and laborers, artists and accountants, moms and mechanics. We are all sent into our world. We are given to those we relate to. We are commissioned to our workplace. We are placed in our streets. When our imaginations grasp our sentness, our life stories take on a whole new, dangerous meaning. As G. A. Studdert Kennedy has said, "Nobody worries about Christ as long as he can be kept shut up in churches. . . . But there is always trouble if you try and let him out." Jesus is not made for staying in churches, and neither are we.

People who may never be on staff or lead an official church ministry can have unleashed imaginations and follow God bravely. Jessica, a mom in Kim's church, is studying social work; her husband, Eric, is a roofer. Jessica embraced her sentness and discovered that God had given her a heart for children in need, so she and Eric stepped up and fostered two more children. In their small, three-bedroom house in the suburbs, they are raising five children. By embracing their sentness they became the hands and feet of Jesus to children in desperate need of care, compassion and a family.

People often like the idea of being sent, but their lives are already full. So they ask us how to create margin for mission. We think there are lots of things someone can do to create rhythms and practices for living a life on mission. However, there is a substantial difference between adding a little missional margin and living sent.

The difference becomes clear when you really understand the famous commission in Matthew 28:18. While most translations have Jesus telling his disciples to "go," the original Greek is closer to "as you go": Jesus is telling his followers, "Make disciples *as you go* about your life." Jessica and Eric do not fit in a little Jesus mission occasionally between soccer games and trips to the mall. They live their sentness every day, in all the little moments.

FROM COUNTRY CLUB TO NIGHTCLUB

Urban Life in Ringwood in Melbourne has been shifting over the last ten years to reinvent their approach to church around their sentness.[6] From the 1970s to the 1990s, the church (then called Christian Life Centre) was a center of charismatic renewal and one of the largest churches in Melbourne. Doug Faircloth, the senior pastor from 1991 to 2005, was curious why the amazing miracles taking place there did not generally translate to concern for others in their city.

Doug, together with an eager group of young adults, dreamed about future options. They asked, "If the church closed tomorrow, would locals miss them?" They walked and prayed around their suburb, asking how people could be served and reached. They invited guest speakers like Alan Hirsch to help them understand what their particular sentness might look like. This group became a transition team, inviting the congregation to contribute their outside-the-box ideas and talk through potential changes and concerns as they shifted toward sentness.

Ultimately they made a dramatic transition, changing the church's location, name, leadership and focus. They relocated from their "country club" acreage to the center of town and renovated an old nightclub into a café and community center—what Frost and Hirsch call a "proximity place"—where Christians could mingle freely with non-Christians.[7] This became an important symbol of who their church is sent to serve as well, as a platform for a range of new ministries. "To live for the well being of our community" became the new mission statement for the newly named "Urban Life," an acronym of "U R Beginning A New Life."

Another radical change at Urban Life was its leadership structure. Doug changed his leadership team from a middle-aged group of elders to an eager group of young adults, and he handed leadership over to Anthea, a young woman who had grown up in Doug's youth group. Anthea had worked as a marketing executive with Disney Corporation, a make-it-happen company that had schooled her in top-down, CEO-styled leadership. She came to realize she needed to unlearn some things and recalibrate to be more empowering and participatory. Inspired by Dorothy in *The Wizard of Oz*, she became a leader who shows compassion to her companions, encourages them to stay on the journey and helps them find strengths within themselves.[8]

Anthea finds fulfillment in being a Dorothy to people around her and helping them see where God is sending them. She is mentoring a young woman, Sharon, who is developing a Myspace site that explores struggles with issues of faith. Some of the language and discussions on that site would offend some church people, but Anthea does not want to smooth too many of Sharon's "rough edges" for fear of "blunting her missional edge." The site is connecting well with people who might never otherwise get involved with a church.

Also at Urban Life are Mary and Owen, who have a passion to reach older people. They started a get-together group for seniors, as well as sponsoring monthly socials, an exercise group, a book club and a Christmas lunch. Local community service organizations refer people to them. Meanwhile, a woman named Roslyn is interested in engaging alternative spirituality seekers with Christian spirituality and charismatic gifts. With Anthea's encouragement, she attended alternative spirituality mind-body-spirit festivals and planned meditation classes at Urban Life. Roslyn's sentness finds her being Christ's witness to people seeking spirituality through all sorts of alternative paths.

Rather than recruiting people to preexisting programs at Urban Life, Anthea's Dorothy-style empowering leadership makes her more likely to ask, "What are your passions? What do you imagine we might do together? And how can we help you fulfill your vision?" For many who have been involved, the Urban Life journey is from being consumer Christians to being missional disciples. Church members become "partners" who identify with the community and support the church's mission. The language of membership, Anthea explains, evokes consumeristic entitlements—the right to vote, for example, or access to special services. Urban Life instead wants to emphasize connective relationships and mutual obligation. Partnership is about serving one another—the person serving the church, the church serving the person—and together pursuing the common mission of living "for the well being of our community."

The most important part of the shift to sentness is not partnership language, physical relocation, branding or leadership changes; the most important part is the redirection outward, in line with *missio Dei*. Anthea says mission has often been reduced to a department of the church, when it is more a description of the character of God. "Christianity is often about populating heaven, where it needs to be about transforming earth." Urban Life maintains an active global interest, especially in Cambodia and Thailand, but the church is careful not to see overseas as the only place of sentness.

The leadership at Urban Life have shifted from waiting for people to come to their church to looking for ways of being sent to their communities. People are adjusting their lifestyle to make time for neighborhood connections and community groups. The worship team had a shortage of singers and musicians as people volunteered more with the soup kitchen and high school ministry. Urban Life defines mission as "being found about our Father's business." The Father's business is sending, and Urban Life wants to cooperate with that. They desire to discern God's heart for a situation and partner with God in mission.

SINCE I AM SENT, DOES THAT MEAN I HAVE TO GO AWAY?

Global mission needs workers who are prepared to relocate to needy areas, especially in the Muslim world and Asia's slums. In different seasons, God calls people to move to bless a new community or to travel to learn something new. But in a world where mobility is so common and easy, we need to consider the call to stability in the places and relationships where God has sent us.

The people of God are not always called to stay, but they are always sent. Sentness is not about taking a plane trip or joining a short-term mission. In fact, when we really understand being sent, we may not *go* anywhere. Jesus called people to leave home and go with him to new places (e.g., Mark 1:16-20)—those people were *sent to go*. But when a man Jesus had delivered of demons asked to join him on his travels, Jesus told him instead to go home and witness there (Mark 5:18-20). He was *sent to stay*.

Perhaps the most extraordinary act of mission and obedience is to stay in your ordinary house and work in your ordinary job *in the name of Jesus*. If your imagination is grabbed by being a sent people, you will see *all* your life as mission.

Darryl Gardiner, who was the director of Youth for Christ New Zealand and has been a long-time mentor and speaker for Forge, was asked to send a team of musicians to Europe for a mission trip. Realizing it would probably not be hard to attract a few musicians looking for an international stage, but wanting to involve the right people, he wrote to a collection of potential candidates. But in his letter of invitation he implied he was looking for those who could give up a fortnight of their time for local outreach and playing in local schools to share about their faith and values. Not everyone replied, and some said no. But a few responded yes. So Darryl brought everyone together and let them know that actually the invitation was for an all-expenses-paid trip to Europe. All of a sudden, some of the musicians who had not been available discovered they could make the time. Some of them were very good musicians, but Daryl already had the team he wanted. Talent was not the only factor; a willingness to be sent, without concern for whether they would be sent someplace mundane or someplace exotic, was a higher priority.

Stability may not be as appealing or imagination grabbing as going overseas or to a remote location. It is less easy to own the identity of "missionary" if we stay where we are. But God wants to send people into their own neighborhoods and networks, suburbs and sports clubs, families and friends. If we grasp that vision, we are indeed missionaries.

SENT TO A TRAILER PARK

The great news about Christianity, the impetus of God's heart, is in the incarnation: Jesus left heaven, came to earth as a person, "moved into the neighborhood" and lived among us (John 1:14 *The Message*). That's why sentness is often also called incarnational mission; we're following Jesus by submerging ourselves incarnationally in our neighborhoods and networks.

Kim Dougherty, a 2011 Forge Chicago resident, discovered her sentness in a trailer park. She had been offering friendship and practical assistance to low-income residents of Woodland Village Mobile Home Park in Wauconda, Illinois.[9] The mobile home park was largely invisible to others in the town. Many did not even know it was there. The park was predominately white but had a growing number of Latino residents. Many lived there while in transition— leaving an abusive relationship, struggling with addictions, managing mental-health issues or looking for work after a felony conviction. Dougherty observed, "Every person I met was determined to be independent and successful, but most couldn't do so."

Dougherty became convinced that God was calling her to a simple expression of mission: be a good neighbor to new friends at Woodland. She had discerned that genuine relationships were a real need in the trailer park community: "Many live isolated and lonely lives that make interacting with people a real challenge. They have few social skills, if any. What they need most is what they are least likely to pursue and least able to supply for themselves." She and her team are committed to integrating with Woodland residents and forming strong relationships.

Dougherty's incarnational move followed an unexpected layoff from Trinity International University. It seemed like a downgrade from her already simple lifestyle. What was different, though, was her missional imagination: she had been captured by the idea that God was sending her to share her life and the love of Christ with her new neighbors—not as an outside visitor but as one of them.

Dougherty did not go with preexisting plans and strategies or with the expectation that she knew what was best for her adopted community. She carefully identified what the community members wanted, what they could do for themselves and what they needed help with. "It is the people living in the community," she says, "who determine what is important in terms of transforming this neighborhood."

Dougherty's team started to explore an area of service they were suited to address: financial and life skills collaboration. But their main focus was simpler than any programs. She said, "I am becoming known in the neighborhood as a trusted friend, not someone coming from outside to impose my will." She and her team give time and priority to doing what good friends do for one another: offering a listening ear, helping coordinate home repairs for neighbors who ask for help, driving others without a car to the grocery store.

One of Dougherty's neighbors lost his job after Illinois cut funding for people with disabilities. A single father of two who has Parkinson's disease, he needed help to get in and out of his home. Dougherty leveraged her connections with churches and a local agency to build him an access ramp. She went further in advocating for him in accessing child support, transportation and other employment, and helped him with the challenges of being a single father. He has since had to move from Woodland, but Dougherty and her Forge team have stayed in contact with him. Sometimes incarnational mission means staying in a geographic area, and sometimes it means staying with a relationship and doing what it takes to help.

Dougherty came to this sense of her sentness while completing a yearlong residency with Forge Chicago. Over the course of the residency she developed a greater sense of what it means to do mission right where she lived.

> American culture is changing rapidly and unless the church adapts its focus and mission strategy, whole generations will be lost. . . . Forge helped me recognize what God was already doing in the world and how I could join him in that work.[10]

NOT PROGRAM BUT POSTURE

A missional imagination sees God at work in the world and joins God in that work, rather than trying to fit mission into our lives and trying to get God to bless it. Mission consultant Alan Roxburgh says,

Rather than the primary question being, "How do we attract people to what we are doing?" it becomes, "What is God already up to in the neighbourhood?" and "What are the ways we need to change in order to engage the people in our community who no longer consider church part of their lives?" This is what a missional imagination is about.[11]

We are convinced that whether a church is missional or not has very little to do with the size of the congregation or whether they have a building or how they worship. Multisite or monastic, chapel or cathedral, alternative or automobile drive-through—take whatever helps you and others connect with God.

You might want your worship leader to come in on a wire from the roof, upside down and spinning, playing the drums with one hand like the drummer from Def Leppard, with machines blowing smoke. Knock yourself out. Or maybe you want to chant, reflect, burn a candle or paint a picture of a person burning a candle while burning a candle. Go for it. We don't really care about style. Kim has co-led a church plant and been on the staff of a large, ten-thousand-person, multisite church. Darren has pastored small, inner-suburban, candle-wielding churches and larger contemporary suburban and regional churches. We have met for church in cafés and pubs, bistros and school halls, parks and pools. We are convinced that in all those settings, a church was at work.

I (Kim) have been involved in training and networking the missional church in Australia and now America. I also helped coach people in a network of house churches. Since being in America, I have been helping several large multisite churches in Chicago and Atlanta adopt a missional posture. At Community Christian Church in Chicago my job title is the director of missional imagination; I help coach leaders and members to adopt the identity of a missionary in their own contexts. Wherever I train people, I do not expect their service style to suit me. I look for what they value and how that is the organizing principle in the church: helping people find their way back to God.

At Forge we encourage everyone to think seriously about their calling to where they already are. Like Kim Dougherty, all Forge residents spend their year actively engaging a specific mission context. For that year we are on mission together—as an apprenticeship for a life of sentness. International mission agencies and mission-minded churches might have maps of the world on their walls; we have maps of our neighborhoods.

There is no program for sentness. There is no nine-week course, no pulling back the curtain on a finely choreographed missional church production, no DVD and workbook series that will change your life. Forge is based on the simple idea of inviting people to rediscover the Jesus of the Gospels, who points to the sending God. When we look at the incarnational Jesus and hear the dangerous stories of those in his kingdom who model his incarnational mission, we are awakened to our sentness, and we step into a new missional life.

DALLAS SENT SPORTSPEOPLE

Ryan Hairston leads the Forge hub in Dallas, Texas, where he has been coaching a young man named Tony. Forge has provided Tony with space to think about following Jesus and joining him in everyday mission, and he has realized that, because he was very busy with church activities, he had few, if any, friendships with people not connected to the church. To join Jesus in mission, Tony saw he needed to invest in relationships with people outside his Christian circles.

Tony did not want to make friends with people just as an excuse to share his faith and invite people to church. He wanted to foster regular, consistent relationships that demonstrated authentic interest and care, relationships that were in fact life giving for him and his friends.

One of Tony's hobbies is exercise, so he decided to join a local gym, engage in their fitness program and see who he might meet along the way. Tony has adopted the gym as his community. Most days of the week he now exercises with a group of about thirty people. When there are gym outings, he joins in.

In the past, if Tony had found time to meet people like his friends from the gym, he would have been preoccupied with how to invite them to church activities. But now he is first asking God to help him see where God is already at work in his friends' lives. He is considering what about the gospel might be considered good news for this group of people.

Can you see the shift? Tony's imagination is captured by what theologians call *prevenient grace*. He is looking for where God is already at work and is keen to cooperate with that. He now sees himself as a missionary, sent into his community to come alongside people and live and share what really is good news. He sees each person not as a project but as someone with particular potential and value, and a particular calling to be all that Jesus wants him or her to be.

As Tony got to know the gym owner, they started sharing a meal about once a week and talking about life. The gym owner is not a follower of Jesus, but he wants to add value to his community and make a difference in the world. Tony has a similar heart for making a difference—it is part of what he understands the kingdom of God to be about. And in hearing the gym owner's heart, Tony felt a nudge from God's Spirit to invite him to join one of his church's projects: fundraising for a well in Africa. The gym owner was thrilled to be involved. Together they dreamed and planned a work-a-thon to add funds to the well project. Tony has come to believe that Jesus wants to invite *everyone* to join in his mission of remaking the world according to God's dream for it; everyone, from Tony's friends at church to his friends at the gym, has value and can play a part in that *missio Dei*.[12]

Laura Hairston, Forge America's executive director, is married (to Ryan) and has two children. Laura participates in a local exercise class and has been developing good relationships with women in the class, most of whom do not attend any church.

Laura is demonstrating good incarnational practice: she has found something she loves to do and seeks to do it with people who are not connected to church. It's almost impossible to have long conversations during exercise, so Laura makes it a priority to relate whenever she can outside class. The best time is going for coffee after class, so Laura visits the local Starbucks after most classes to catch up on everyone's news.

At one of these post-exercise coffee chats, one of the women expressed concern about her clashes with her teenage daughter. She said she would love it if an older woman could mentor her daughter. With an open invitation to share in the life of this family, and a nudge from the Holy Spirit, Laura gladly offered.

The mom was excited, and before long other moms were asking the same question, and Laura was mentoring eight other daughters— only two of whom had a faith background. The girls were open to studying the Bible together, and they are beginning to be open to Jesus. The moms appreciate the difference Laura and the group are making for their girls, and they've asked Laura to do something similar with them.[13]

"God Knew—Right, Dad?"

Sentness is not a new program but a posture of availability to God and engagement with the lives of people around us. As such, it's not just good for the people we meet; it's also good for us. We think all Christians and people in ministry need the balance of engaging with the world around them. We love the exercise and friendships, conversations and fun that come from regular engagement in sporting communities and friendship circles outside the church. It is good for the body and good for the soul. It puts us in touch with people we would not meet otherwise. It exposes us to different perspectives and helps us understand how people outside the church, or with different faith perspectives or none, see the world.

Since I (Kim) was a kid, my goal had been to live in America. But I could never have imagined that I would preach at, let alone join the staff of, one of the fastest-growing churches in America. In 2009 our family packed ten suitcases and moved to the United States so that I could join the team at Community Christian Church to help mobilize the entire church into a missional posture. I was also given the humbling privilege of serving alongside Alan Hirsch, one of my lifelong heroes and mentors, as the national director of Forge America.

We left Australia in December. That's summer in Australia, with an average temperature that year of 110 degrees. When we landed in Chicago, every square inch of our new homeland was a winter wonderland. It was like Narnia without Aslan. I love the snow, though; I am big and purpose-built for it. Actually we all love the snow. So all five of us dove into it. My three boys built snowmen and threw snowballs.

Our host family, the warm and generous Warners, helped us transition into this strange and wonderful country. Even though we were living in a basement nearly ten thousand miles away from friends and family, we huddled around our newly decorated Christmas tree, the five of us as a family, embracing our sentness.

Our cozy, picturesque experience did not last long. Four weeks later our seven-year-old son, Carter, started to complain that he was out of breath and his heart was beating fast. With the move and the snow and all, it was only that day that we noticed, for the first time, that he looked *really* pale and had red spots on his legs.

We took him to the doctor, who immediately did blood work. I will never forget when my wife, Maria, arrived at our house as her cell phone rang. It was the doctor, confirming our greatest fears: Carter had cancer—childhood acute lymphoblastic leukemia (ALL). We both felt sick to our core.

The doctor said he would call an ambulance, but we did not wait. We bundled our little boy into the back of our car and drove as fast as we could to the University of Chicago. With the ink barely dry on the health insurance policy, my little boy was put onto a stretcher and wheeled into the emergency room, where he went through eight life-saving blood transfusions.

Over the next three and half years, the cancer continued to torture Carter. He had spinal taps and bone marrow scrapes. A port was put into his chest for chemo, and doctors explained that his hair would fall out and his gums would bleed and be filled with ulcers. He was nauseated; his feet hurt; there were many days he would just sleep.

In Australia, we would have had access to free health care and a network of care from an entire community who loved us and knew Carter from when he was a baby. Carter had not made any American friends yet when the battle started. All our family lived on the other side of the world. I wept. I cried every day. I cried out to God, *Please, please don't let my little boy die.* I did not have any big fancy prayers—just tears. Years later, I still cry, just a little less.

Our oldest son, Lachlan, is a beautiful boy with a heart for God and people—so much so that Maria took him with her on her last trip to Cambodia before cancer changed our life.[14] So it is not surprising that ten-year-old Lachlan's comments would affect us as much as they did. After Carter's diagnosis, Lachlan came into the hospital room and held my hand. "God knew—right, Dad?"

"Knew what?" I asked.

"That we are meant to be here, to stay? Because Carter would have got cancer in Australia if we were meant to stay there, and we would never have come. So we are staying, because God sent us here, aren't we, Dad?"

Staying. We were here, together as a sent family. And so we stayed. And we cried. The first three years in America were the most fulfilling of our lives, but also the saddest and hardest season we have ever gone through as a family.

You may think we are crazy. And we may be. When we embrace our sentness, God does not promise us smooth sailing. There are no Lamborghinis and rainbows every day like some preachers promise. God doesn't promise that; he does promise, however, never to leave us. God weeps with us, and we are not alone in our grief and pain.

After three years, two months and six days of chemotherapy, Carter is cancer-free and beginning a new chapter of his life—in America, where God sent us, where we stayed.

Being sent is about staying because we are called. Obviously there are some circumstances where people in risk and danger need to move; there are dangerous, abusive places that God most definitely does not send us to or ask us to stay in. Most of us in the Western world, however, need to recognize that the best missionaries for our work, school, street or business are us. We need to celebrate that our very backyards are mission fields and that we are sent there to stay.

The Bible is full of examples that those who stayed and embraced their sentness, no matter what the circumstances, are the ones who finished the race and finished well. God was able to move through them in a powerful way, no matter how broken they were. In fact, the more broken we are, the more God seems to use us: as Reverend T. D. Jakes has said, "It is only broken bread that is given to the body of Christ by Jesus." Anyone can stay in comfort and peace, but when someone chooses to stay—to bless, to minister, to be the church—through trial and suffering, that choice becomes evidence of God's love for the people around them.

If there is one posture that is nonnegotiable, if there is one that sets all the others in motion, it is the posture of being sent. Sentness is in our DNA. We are all sent—not some, not a special few, not just the ordained, not just those with degrees. Sentness is for everyone and anyone who accepts the free gift of grace and dares to follow Jesus.

If you are asking why being sent is so important, or if you are cynical that missional Christianity is just a trend, let me say this: God sent the Son, who came and lived and served and died and rose again to ascend to the right hand of the Father. The Father and Son don't leave us alone but rather send the Holy Spirit to help us in our sentness. This sentness is not about some new trend. It's the heartbeat of *missio Dei*, the *sent God*.

We stayed. If we can do it, you can too. God will use you to be salt and light in dark places, even in your darkest hour. You will become more like Jesus in the process of obedience and trust, and you will look back and see how God used the journey and not just the destination. While others change jobs, marriages, houses and churches, always consuming and never settling, you will be growing and being used by God as part of his greater design.

3

SUBMERGED MINISTRY

So the Word became human and made his home among us.
He was full of unfailing love and faithfulness.
And we have seen his glory, the glory of
the Father's one and only Son.

JOHN 1:14

Our churches, under the guise of doing the work of Christ,
are inadvertently sucking us away from the very people that Jesus
would want us to hang out with. . . . Read the dangerous stories in
the Gospels . . . of the one who was accused by religious people
of being a drunkard and a glutton. I'm convinced that
those stories, if taken seriously, will propel you
out of organized Christianity and into the
third places in your neighbourhood.

MICHAEL FROST

EVEN THOUGH OUR FAMILY is new to the United States, I (Kim) have always loved American culture. Coming here and submerging ourselves in American life is more a privilege than a chore. I am a proud Australian, but I moved to America partly because I have always deeply loved America and Americans. Back in Australia, our family celebrated July 4. We set off fireworks and flew the American flag. I love America holidays and celebrations like Thanksgiving.

I am sure there are times Americans don't believe me. So I tell them that we named our second son, Carter, after a character on the American TV show *ER*. We named our third son, Jordan, after Chicago Bulls legend Michael Jordan. To seal the proof of my patriotism, I show them the American flag on my Bank of America Visa card. Only real patriots have an American flag on their Visa card!

Some adjustments to life in America have been hard. It's a different country. It's hard to adjust to polarizing politics, for example. I have also found it difficult getting used to some of the language. You say, "Put it in the trunk," and we say, "Put it in the boot." You say trash can, we say rubbish bin. You say fries, we say chips. Most of this is fine. But on a trip to a water park, I asked a shopkeeper for "some thongs, size eight, preferably in black, for me. And give me some rainbow ones as well." I thought she was going to call security. In Australia, we wear thongs on our feet at the beach, but obviously *thongs* means something different in America.

It goes the other way as well. When we moved here, everyone was telling me, "I'm rooting for you." In Australia this means dirty, nasty sex. I did not want to know that the business manager at work was rooting for me. My boss had to send out an email asking for everyone to please stop sending me messages about rooting.[1] But all the confusion notwithstanding, I love where God has sent us for this season of our lives.

America is so diverse. I went down South, which I loved, and saw people dressed in Confederate uniforms and flying the Confederate flag. I wondered what African American people thought of that. Isn't the Confederate flag offensive to them? Didn't the South lose the Civil War? I asked a Southern pastor, and he told me it's complicated. Also complicated is San Francisco—a beautiful city, but to this Greek Australian immigrant educated in a Christian school, a strange place. When I was there last, the front page of the newspaper had an article debating whether people who ride their bike to work naked and stop at a café should be made to put a modesty towel on their chair. The article is not debating whether they should wear clothes, but whether they should be forced to use towels out of respect for others who might sit on the chairs after them. There is nowhere in Australia where you could ride a bike naked. You would be tasered and arrested.

We can never say the gospel can be translated the same way in all places. Dave Ferguson, lead pastor at Community Christian Church in Chicago and chairman of the largest church-planting conference in the world,[2] says that we cannot assume our models for mission will work everywhere. In Melbourne I was part of The Junction, a grassroots network of missional communities, and now I am part of America's largest multisite church. But in both contexts, we have to start with asking where God is at work.

Maria and I had the choice to live anywhere in America, but we were called to Aurora, the poorest, predominantly Latino area in Illinois. Our area, Hometown, is 80 percent Latino; affordable houses here start at $60,000. The Aurora police have arrested twenty Latino Kings gang leaders. Our neighborhood is struggling. Many people who live here bought homes for $200,000 that are now worth less than $100,000. It has the third-worst school system in the country. Its violence is unparalleled. Our local 7-Eleven convenience store was being robbed every week. We were amazed to find out that a Christian developer, Perry Bigalow, built Hometown with a vision for Christian community. He designed the roads so you could walk or bike around, not just drive. And the post office is the center of town.

We moved to Hometown intentionally to join friends and a number of families from our church. We did not want to just lecture and talk about local mission, but do it. We prayed together, "Where are you at work, God, and where can we join you?" Locals pay fifty dollars a month to the homeowners association for lawn mowing and other caretaking. But there were no longer any community events sponsored by the association; many people hated living there and had given up on building a better community. So Maria and I, with a group of friends, offered to get events going again.

We asked, "What do the kids like to do?" They love playing baseball and soccer, so we offered to teach sports. Ninety kids came out. Now, I am a fat, second-generation Greek Aussie immigrant. My united eyebrow is a giveaway of my ethnic heritage. When I taught baseball, the kids ended up hitting the baseball like they were using a cricket bat. No one cared, though, and there were plenty of other families teaching. Parents brought lawn chairs to watch us teach, because it so entertaining. Our team grew and eventually one family, the Moberlys, who had lived there since the neighborhood first started, took over leading that missional activity.

We also asked questions like "What's your big holiday?" July 4 was big for Hometown, so we put on a July 4 party. Five hundred people were involved. Out of those connections and relationships, we have started two small groups.

We have stayed and submerged ourselves here because we were sent. We don't just do community development because it's a good idea. We don't do it to grow numbers in a big church in another suburb. We identify strongly with our community and want to be good news and life for our neighbors.

Missional church is not about programs. God is more committed than we are to prison ministry or schools ministry or neighborhood house churches or whatever ministry we get involved in. We don't ask God to bless our program; we ask God where he is at work, and we find ways to join in.

TO SUBMERGE IS TO BECOME VULNERABLE

The 2000 movie *Chocolat* is set in the imagined French Catholic town of Lansquenet in 1959. Vianne Rocher (played by Juliette Binoche) is a young, single mother who enters the town as an outsider. She blows in with the wind and opens a chocolaterie just as Lent starts. Vianne's chocolate and her friendship and hospitality help people reclaim unfulfilled dreams, reconcile with estranged friends and relatives, and stand up for a life worth living. With her lovely and tasty chocolate creations, she offers permission to indulge.

Of course, this chocolaterie stands in contrast to the Catholic Church's teaching on abstinence and denial, especially during Lent. Vianne's nemesis is the town mayor, who stands for tradition and moral rigidness.[3] The mayor and a likeable priest (the puppet of the mayor, suggestive of Christendom's entanglement of church and state) resist Vianne's offer of chocolate, the changes it brings and what it stands for. Other characters are also resentful, especially Serge, an abusive husband. Vianne helps his wife, Josephine, by offering her alternative lodging and work in the chocolaterie. Serge reacts angrily, burning the boat that Vianne's romantic interest has floated into town on.

Worn out and feeling driven off, Vianne is almost ready to move on. But Vianne's daughter is tired of relocating and urges her toward stability. Ultimately her hope is restored when the mayor succumbs to stuffing himself with chocolate in her store, and her friends surprise her by making chocolates for an Easter Sunday celebration.

The town helps bring healing to Vianne, just as she has brought more holistic perspectives to the town.

Vianne is not only a redemptive force in this film; she also experiences redemption. We learn from Vianne to love life and help others to love life, laugh often, savor the moment and make life-giving choices. But we also learn that to be submerged in a community is to become vulnerable. In our sentness, we experience mutuality in ministry. The place heals the missionary even as the missionary works at healing the place. These are lessons we learn from Jesus too.

JESUS SAVES THE PARTY

When I (Kim) was confirmed in the Catholic Church, my mom gave me a picture of Jesus. The picture was special to me, but I was terrified of it. Jesus wore a white robe, looked perfect, without blemish, and stared at me. He made a creepy Vulcan sign with one hand and in the other held a bow that suggested to me he was ready to kill me if I sinned. Lying on his back was a lamb—which made sense, since Jesus was a shepherd—but the lamb looked dead, with its neck broken. I imagined that would be me if I sinned.

I put a teddy bear in front of Jesus so he wouldn't stare at me all the time. I longed to follow God, but I had to follow him from a distance. I dared not get close, in case he sensed my sin.

One of my (Darren's) earliest pictures of Jesus came in a nice, literal frame from my Nana. You might recognize it—the bearded, ladylike Jesus of Nana's picture can be found on many Sunday school walls. With blue eyes and blond hair, unlike anyone born in Palestine for hundreds of years before or after, this Jesus looks into the distance with the sun shining on his face. He looks inoffensive, unflappable, even spooky. Nana's Jesus picture was domesticated, a "break-glass-in-case-of-emergency" Jesus.

We have been getting a different picture of Jesus from rereading the Gospels and reflecting on the book *ReJesus*. There Alan Hirsch and Mike Frost portray Jesus as radical, wild, dangerous, mysterious, with an agenda often different from our own.[4] The Jesus from our childhood pictures doesn't look much like that. He doesn't look like someone who might bartend either. But for his first public miracle—his first missionary act—he did exactly that.

Jesus was enjoying a moment of festivity at a wedding with family and friends when his mom asked him a favor. Weddings in Jesus' day were different from today's. Our weddings are usually half a day, with a reception at night. In Jesus' time, they were seven-day events. This community feast of the newlyweds started and ended with wine that the father of the bride provided.

When a daughter was born, after getting over the initial disappointment of having a girl, the father would draw off one barrel of wine in preparation for her wedding. Each birthday he would set aside another barrel. Assuming he was a good father, on the eve of the wedding feast he would have fifteen or more barrels of wine.

The wedding we read of in John 2 took place in Cana. It was a naughty northern wedding, far away from the center of respected society, the Jerusalem temple and religious headquarters. Before long, there were two noteworthy empty containers at this wedding. The Jewish people of Jesus' day had an ancient ritual of elaborate and purposeful hand washing that made them ceremonially clean, separating them in God's eyes from the sinful Gentiles and making them sacred. There must have been a lot of hand washing going on at this wedding, because the sacred stone jars stood empty, a stark reminder of the divide between those who were in and those who were out, those who were spiritual and those who were not, the sacred and the secular, the holy and the unholy. There were not too many holy people at this wedding.

The religious jars were not the only empty containers at the wedding. Mary, the attentive Jewish mother, noticed that the wine barrels were empty; the party had run out of wine. There are only two logical reasons you run out of wine during a wedding: (1) the father has shamed his family and daughter by not drawing enough off every year, or (2) they were all a little thirsty and had drunk too much too fast. We do not know why or how or when the wine ran out, but we do know that Mary asked Jesus to do something about it.

Jesus could have taken the opportunity to expose the stinginess of the bride's father. He could have stood up on the platform and chastened the wedding guests for overdrinking. He could have announced, "You should be ashamed of yourselves." That is how many religious people act.

But Jesus knew that to move into a neighborhood and live an authentically spiritual life there meant being present and generous with neighbors. Jesus' approach was to embrace those he was sent to. And he did this with surprising graciousness. Jesus knew how to bring everyday spirituality to a party without condoning and without condemning. He laughed out loud and often, and he included others in his enjoyment of culture and of good food, wine and friends. He could be a part of the party without condoning drunkenness, but also without condemning the partygoers. Jesus was surrounded by the most sinful people he could be with, but instead of condemning them, he showed his glory in the most ordinary way.

Jesus brought those two empty things together—the empty religious jars and the empty wine barrels—and turned them into a profound lesson, for the disciples and for us.

Jesus asked the attendants to fill the empty ceremonial jars with water. Then he asked them to take some to the master of ceremonies. The most delicious wine passed through his lips. The master of ceremonies, who did not know what had happened but enjoyed the results, honored the father by saying to the bridegroom, "Sir, most people use the oldest wine first, but you are a connoisseur, and you have saved the best till last."

This is a dangerous story. Jesus' first miracle was not at the center of society, in Jerusalem or anywhere near the temple. It was in the North, in Cana, at a party. Jesus took symbols of exclusion and used them to lubricate a party. He took the cold stone jars of religious separation and filled them with wine. And in an act of incredible generosity and graciousness, it was the best wine. Jesus does things like that, and we love that about him.

This is not the sort of thing we imagine Christians doing. A lot of Christians do not know how to act at a wedding; many religious people will not even go to a wedding party. They might see it as a conflict of interest or be too busy with other activities. They might associate alcohol with addiction and violence. But the Lord, who never sinned and was a friend of sinners, could go to a wedding at Cana. And in the middle of that place, which seemed far from sacred and holy, he showed his presence and generosity with a miracle that was a sign of his glory (John 2:11). This event announced that the kingdom of God was coming, the wedding banquet Isaiah had prophesied about thousands of years before in his announcement of the Messiah. And John tells us that display of generosity and messianic spirituality led his disciples to put their faith in him.

We love the mutuality of Jesus' ministry that plays out here as well. Jesus is influenced by Mary in this story; he doesn't just act unilaterally and symbolically—he responds to an immediate and normal need as a member of a larger community. He becomes vulnerable, subject to, committed to the particularity of the place he has been sent. He is marinating in the culture, taking on its flavor, even as he himself seasons it.

That is the Jesus we want to follow, not just from a distance but in his footsteps. We need Jesus' laughter, his sheer love of life and his infectious holiness. That is how Jesus calls us to live.

Jesus' spirituality was not only concerned with the so-called sacred aspects of life. Spirituality modeled on Jesus requires loving

God, loving people and celebrating the goodness of God's gifts in all areas of life. It means being salt and light in the marketplace and the neighborhood, bringing generosity and grace, laughing loud and often and bearing witness to Jesus' goodness so that people ask us why we have hope.

Michael Frost preached about this dangerous story of Jesus at Cana as part of Kim's 2002 Forge residency.[5] It is a profound story that we have been living into and preaching about since. Like much of what Jesus said and did, it is a profound paradigm change. Jesus' example challenges us to consider where Cana is in our context. Do we shop in our Cana? Do we send our kids to school there and go to weddings there? Do we give priority to partying with our friends and neighbors when there are things to celebrate? And if our neighborhood has not had a party for a while, do we look for things to celebrate?

These are the sort of questions we ask ourselves; they drive many conversations during Forge residencies. They are paradigm-changing questions prompted by taking a fresh look at Jesus.

WHAT WOULD JESUS BREW?

"What would Jesus do (WWJD)?" becomes a very challenging question when we think about the sorts of things Jesus did. Unfortunately, WWJD? can be narrowly used, only in relation to personal morality. We prefer asking, "What is Jesus doing (WIJD)?" so we can join in with what the risen and alive Jesus is up to.

When he was raising funds for some community development projects out of Third Place Communities in Tasmania, Australia, our friend Darryn Altclass made some T-shirts to sell. Printed on them were the words "What would Jesus brew?" At one level he was urging people to think about what caffeinated or alcoholic beverages Jesus might drink with friends or, more importantly, to realize that Jesus would hang out and drink something with friends. But at another level he was also asking people to think about what Jesus was brewing and fostering in their local community. "What is Jesus brewing here?"

Opening our eyes to what Jesus is brewing is aided by an understanding of *missio Dei*. It is not that the church has a mission but that God has a mission in which he invites the church to cooperate. Also helpful is the notion of prevenient grace, the conviction that God's grace is present in the world, its cultures and its people before missionaries arrive on the scene. We are sent, but Jesus goes ahead of us. It is up to us to ask and discern what God is doing, what Jesus is brewing, so we can join in.[6] This is what singer Bono says has captured his imagination: "Stop asking God to bless what you're doing. Find out what God's doing. It's already blessed."[7]

DANCES WITH LOCALS

I (Darren) have identified three key ingredients of a great movie epic: romance, culture and horses. My wife, Jenni, knows this about me and has bought me the 1990 movie *Dances with Wolves*—three times! The movie depicts Union Army Lieutenant John Dunbar (played by Kevin Costner) taking a post at Fort Sedgwick. Desiring to see the American frontier before it disappears, he finds Fort Sedgwick abandoned, leaving him the challenge of rebuilding in solitude. He records his observations in a journal. At first his neighbors, the local Lakota Indians, keep their distance and try to scare him off. But when he helps them find an injured tribe member, Stands with a Fist (whom he eventually falls in love with), he starts to build bridges of understanding with them. Dunbar befriends a wolf that he names Two Socks. Seeing him prance around with Two Socks, the Lakota give Dunbar the name Dances with Wolves.

Dunbar gradually learns the Lakota language and grows to respect their culture. But they remain mistrusting and debate what to do with this stranger. A turning point comes one evening when the tribe is ceremonially dancing and Dunbar joins them unannounced. He is initially attacked and dragged off his horse as an intruder into their sacred space. But when the tribe realizes he is advocating for them, announcing he has found the coveted buffalo herds, he joins the hunt and then the dance of the tribe.

Ultimately Dunbar adopts the tribe's ways and is adopted into it. His respect for his adopted culture and advocacy for the people he comes to call his own inspires us to dance with locals in our cultures.[8]

One person we know who dances with locals as part of his sentness is Vincent Donovan. Sent as a traditional medical and teaching missionary to the Masai people in Tanzania, his ministry was initially consumed with asking for land for buildings and using Western technology and finances. But out of frustration with his lack of effectiveness, he stopped doing all that and sat and talked with the locals about God. What a novel idea for a missionary! Vincent would tell a story to someone, ask him or her to pass it on to others and then ask the community to respond and explore what the gospel meant for them. In this dance, he saw himself as a learner and then a facilitator of ongoing and mutual learning.

> I told them I believed that they knew God long before we came, and that they were a devout and very pious people in the face of God. It was not our belief that God loves us Christians more than them, nor that God had abandoned them or forgotten them until we came along. From the beginning it was evident that we were going to have to learn from them as well as teach them.[9]

Donovan was following in the steps of Jesus, who had "moved into the neighborhood" (John 1:14 *The Message*), and Paul and other gospel communicators whose communication emerged from their conversational dances with locals. Mission, at its best, is a mutual and sensitive exchange and partnership—just like dancing.

Most Christians are good hearted and want to be open to God's leading in new directions, but we need our experiences broadened beyond church as we have always known it. Darren's denominational tribe, the Baptist Union of Victoria, developed a congregational resource, *Out of the Box*, to guide churches to practice new approaches for fostering a missional imagination and engaging the broader community. Among the valuable exercises in *Out of the Box* are prayer walks around a neighborhood with a guided group process. Another is inviting what may be provocative input from the local mayor, indigenous or refugee group leaders, and visitors without church backgrounds.

As you ask questions and listen to people's experiences and perceptions of God, keep in mind that you are cooperating with God in *missio Dei*. The Spirit of God is active in drawing people to Jesus. Part of our role, as evangelist Rick Richardson suggests, is to be junior partners in the detective agency of the Holy Spirit, not preachers with agendas but travel guides joining people on their journey and story listeners and storytellers.[10] When I (Kim) was pastoring at The Junction, I often worked and had meetings in cafés. One morning our waitress asked how our church started projects. She had a dream, she explained, of organizing a function to help respond to global poverty. She wondered if I might be able to help with advice. She was thrilled when I said we would love to be involved.

When we embrace our sentness, we engage our neighbors in ways that consumer churches wouldn't naturally consider. We cooperate with God in exploring how he is inviting a person to respond to the good news of Jesus. It is our role to ask questions and be attentive so we can discern and celebrate what God is doing.

TAMPA UNDERGROUND

Brian Sanders started the Underground in Ebor in inner-city Tampa, Florida, in 2006 with a team of friends. Their name is a sign of respect to the underground church throughout history, marked by sacrificial faith in the context of oppression, danger and martyrdom. It is their heart to represent that heritage in their city. Underground is actually a community or network of small missional groups, or microchurches.

Sanders observes that many people who have walked away from church, or at least their experience of church, are actually on a quest to be the body of Christ. Many of them found traditional church services tedious, an endless cycle of sameness. The Underground started with the desire to reconnect with New Testament passion and to have a fresh imagination for mission.[11]

Underground groups gather for a Sunday morning "Crucible" service, but the main action is in the microchurches. Each has its own identity and mission. For example, there are mission-based microchurches shaped around dance and craft, campus-based university groups, and groups seeking to reach particular populations, such as Latinos, artists, men, abused women or sex workers:

- "Mama Africana" offers mentoring in ethnic identity and faith development to black girls.

- "Hoola for Happiness" takes hula hoops to unreached people groups around the world.

- "Links of Hope" teaches jewelry making and microenterprise development to women on the margins and to deaf children.

- "The [Timothy] Initiative" gives work experience to the homeless or unemployed.

- "The Pink House" offers accommodation for families in crisis.

- "The Well" offers meals and conversation to neighbors in need.

With a passion for the poor and people at the margins of the church as we know it, the Underground is convinced that discipleship and community happen best for a group as they are engaged together in mission. They value sincere worship, character-based leadership, generous giving and the pursuit of the Spirit's gifts—all with the priority of accomplishing their part in the mission of God. Underground staff, training, Sunday services and facilities all empower believers to know God's heart and their unique calling to meet needs and proclaim the good news. They do not have a high view of the church as an institution but do have a high view of the church's "kingdom mission," as they state in their manifesto:

> We believe that healing comes through offering healing to others, that discipleship does not primarily take place in a lecture but through doing. We believe that intimacy with God comes from being in his presence and through submission to His will, by doing what He is doing. Since we believe that the life of Jesus and the early church demonstrate that God himself is with the lost and the poor of the earth, proclaiming the good news of His kingdom, we also believe that when we co-labor with Him as workers in that harvest field, we not only bring the kingdom into that place, but that we also experience the deepest and truest intimacy with God.[12]

Underground started with fifty people in seven groups. The groups have mushroomed in number to more than sixty in Tampa and have spread into emerging global movements in Haiti, Manila and Hamburg. Microchurches are not franchise groups but locally contextualized communities submerging deeply in their neighborhoods and networks to bring revolutionary transformation. Underground pastors have adopted a permission-giving and empowering approach to starting new groups. They do not plan the next microchurch as much as ask people what their vision is and how they can empower and facilitate it. This is what submerged spirituality sounds like: we are close to God when we are close to the people God has sent us to. Our God-given distinctiveness is highlighted when we are planted—submerged into the earth, like a seed— among the people God calls us to.

PULPIT TO FIRE STATION

Michael Banes made a dramatic career change to fully live a life of mission.[13] He had been a pastor for twenty-five years, but realized—and grew increasingly uncomfortable with the fact—that he did not really know any people that were not from church. So he left his work as a pastor and applied to the fire department. He currently serves as a professional firefighter in Joplin, Missouri, and he views every day on the job as a chance to love and serve people and point them to the gospel.

On the wall of his home Michael has two "Firefighter of the Year" awards. Given through a peer-based voting process, one of the awards is from 2005 and the other from 2012. That is not bad, seeing that Michael is in his fifties, working in a young man's industry. And he revels in it. He enjoys being like a father or older brother to a bunch of much younger men.

First responders have their own language, rhythms of work and play. They work twenty-four hours on and have forty-eight hours off, so it is hard to get them to church. They often experience trauma and life-threating situations as part of their job. Joplin in particular has recent experience of such trauma; in 2011, Joplin was hit by an F5 tornado that killed 158 people and injured more than 1,100. It was the deadliest tornado in America since 1947. Michael, his nephew Clarke (who was an ambulance emergency medical technician) and their wives have taken their missional context seriously. They have fully moved into the neighborhood. Clarke's wife, Carrisa, sees her job as an emergency-room nurse as her mission field. In fact, through their work they were introduced to two girls they fostered and then adopted.

In 2013, Michael changed to volunteer status with the fire department and became a communications officer for the Carthage Police Department. The department chief had seen Michael's incarnational influence in the firefighting community and created the position to allow him to influence the law enforcement culture.

Mission is not just about going; it is about submerging, staying when things are tough and sticking around when others leave. It's also about listening to God and the community, and stepping into roles that God might prepare in advance for you to do.

ARCHBISHOP FREIER

Philip Freier came to Melbourne, Australia, as the Anglican archbishop in 2007. He was eager not to get absorbed in committees and institutional work; he wanted his ministry to emerge out of engagement with the broader community of Melbourne. So he submerged himself in Prayer4Melbourne Quest. Freier sought conversations in universities, shops, workplaces, blogs, his Federation Square Breakfast Conversations and public lectures. His community engagement in public spaces includes listening to both the strong and influential and the uncertain and troubled. Prayer4Melbourne Quest has helped him understand and engage pressing public issues, especially loneliness, homelessness, fear of strangers, the marginalization of indigenous Australians, the state of childhood, support for people with disabilities and their aging parents, climate change and global poverty.

A particular prayer for Melbourne emerged for Freier out of this Quest:

> God of community,
> we give you thanks for this beautiful and vibrant city:
> for its diversity of people and cultural life,
> for its industry and commerce,
> for its hospitals and agencies of care,
> and for its places of learning, recreation and worship.
> God of compassion,
> we pray for all who live and work in this city and for those
>   who visit here:

open our hearts to
  welcome the stranger,
  shelter the homeless,
  befriend the lonely,
  care for the needy,
  and offer hope to those in despair. . . .
God of community,
Giver of life, of love and hope,
Hear our prayers for the welfare of this city. Amen.[14]

This kind of heartfelt prayer comes only from submerging ourselves in a local community. It is missional spirituality at its best.

GOD NEXT DOOR

Becoming someone who dances with locals is integral to joining the mission of God in our neighborhoods. And it's fun. We love our neighborhoods; we shop there, drink coffee, get to know shopkeepers and fellow customers, and see friends of our kids at the shops and parks. Most weeks (or maybe it's most days) we enjoy a morning coffee at a local shop. Our best Saturdays are spent going to our kids' sports events and learning how other parents see the world.

We want our churches not just to understand the Bible, but also to understand our local communities. What are our neighborhoods really saying? What makes them tick? What drives people's ambitions and directions in life? What is it that holds the community together? How do we start this dance of local community engagement? In his book *God Next Door* Simon Holt, senior minister at Collins Street Baptist Church in Melbourne, suggests practices for engaging neighborhoods as part of spirituality and mission, such as

- dawdling in the street
- exegeting the neighborhood

- celebrating with neighborhood parties and liturgies
- being counterculturally stable
- prayer walking[15]

Holt and others can articulate more developed approaches to community engagement and community development. But we start with walking around, getting to know our communities and neighbors, and getting in step with local rhythms.

COMMUNALITY

At its best locally, mission is not especially exotic. Maria and I (Kim) don't house-share beyond our nuclear family, and we are not church planting among gay, goth, church-burning neo-Marxists. We don't live in an urban slum. But our eyes have been opened to the poverty in the suburbs where we have lived. From the moment we got married, we saw food and hospitality as ways we could embrace our sentness. For us, *missio Dei* involves barbecues, babysitting and basketball.

Similarly, Jenni and I (Darren) are passionate about discerning where God is in our inner-suburban, family-raising, career-pursuing, bike-riding, kitchen-renovating, multicultural, university neighborhood. Submerging ourselves in our neighborhoods is a foundational posture of sentness.

Michael Frost suggests that one of the most neglected skills of church planters is listening. Just as Jesus listened to the crowds, as we submerge ourselves in ministry, we need to listen to the cries and hopes of people we meet.[16]

Geoff Maddock is an Australian married to a Southern belle named Sherry. After Sherry completed a master's degree in exercise physiology at Wake Forest University and Geoff completed a bachelor's in criminology at Melbourne University, they decided to go to Asbury Seminary and get degrees in missiology. They were open to being sent to the other side of the world, but instead felt called to their adopted community in Lexington, Kentucky. They joined John Smith and some other students to found Communality, one of several New Monastic communities in the United States. They moved into inner-city neighborhoods that have issues of drugs and violence. They bought homes right in the middle of these forgotten areas.

Words do not do justice to the way the Maddocks love their community. We are convinced this is how Jesus would live in Lexington. The Maddocks are avid gardeners—more like urban farmers. We like to tease them by calling them hippies. When the crack house next door to their home burnt down, they acquired the land and began to raise chickens and bees and vegetables that we can't even name and that Kim definitely won't eat. With their ten-year-old son, Isaac, the Maddocks are delighted to be caught up in the slow work of submerging in a place, cultivating community and flourishing in crosscultural mission.

As we (Kim and Maria) drove the streets of the neighborhood, Geoff and Sherry told us with great description and enthusiasm the stories of those who live in certain houses, play in the parks and are the local artists, heroes and elders. These are their friends and neighbors. On different streets you'll find other members of Communality embedded into every part of the life of the neighborhood. The Maddocks occasionally share their time with missionaries and churches; teams can spend a week with them learning their model for Christian formation in missional engagement. Alan Hirsch recently spent some time there and came back profoundly affected, describing it as a deeply spiritual experience in what many would consider a grubby, ordinary, poor, urban neighborhood.[17]

Sometimes it is easier to adopt the identity of a missionary and the posture of the incarnation when we are sent to the ends of the

earth, but the missionary calling is for all of us who follow Jesus.
The foundation of missional imagination is to see ourselves as missionaries—not just when we are sent overseas but when Jesus sends
us to our neighborhoods and networks to submerge—in the same
way the Father sent him.

4

SHALOM SPIRITUALITY

The most important commandment is this: "Listen, O Israel!
The LORD our God is the one and only LORD. And you must love the
LORD your God with all your heart, all your soul, all your mind,
and all your strength." The second is equally important:
"Love your neighbor as yourself." No other
commandment is greater than these.

JESUS (MARK 12:29-31)

One worships more fully, prays more deeply, and studies
more diligently when all is done in the context
of a life of action and spiritual momentum.

MICHAEL FROST AND ALAN HIRSCH

IN THE **1987** MOVIE *Babette's Feast* two sisters, Martine and
Philippa, live in a small village in nineteenth-century Denmark
with their father, a respected pastor of a small church. Martine and

Philippa both have marriage opportunities that would allow them to leave the village, but they choose to stay with their father, who discourages marriage. The three of them serve their dwindling and aging congregation together.

Decades later Babette, a French refugee from Paris, begs to work as their housekeeper and cook. She is accepted into the lives of the family and others in their village as she cooks for them for fourteen years.

When the father dies, the sisters plan a dinner to celebrate the hundredth anniversary of his birth. Babette has won enough money from a lottery ticket to return to her previous lifestyle, but she stays and offers to prepare the special meal. She goes all-out in creating a luscious banquet, secretly spending all her winnings to provide a "real French dinner" with ingredients from the best of Paris in appreciation for the welcoming and safe space the family had given her. The dishes are lavish and colorful: turtle soup, caviar, quail, walnut salad, blue cheese and fruit, and rum sponge cake. Babette has even bought beautiful china and linen to set a stylish table.

The sisters and the congregation, however, are nervous about what French Catholic Babette is arranging. They are concerned it may be a sensual sin or perhaps some form of devilry to eat it. They decide that they will not speak about the food or its pleasures during the meal.

Martine's old suitor, now a married general, returns to town for the meal. Not being a part of the conspiracy of non-enjoyment, he comments generously on the food and rare wines, and compares it to a meal he had enjoyed years before at the famous Café Anglais in Paris. It is revealed that Babette was formerly the chef of Café Anglais. She explains a dinner for twelve at Café Anglais would cost ten thousand francs.

The sisters think Babette will return to Paris, but her money is now gone; she is not going anywhere. Martine tearfully says, "Now you will be poor the rest of your life."

Babette proudly replies, "An artist is never poor."

Babette's meal was an act of shalom—an extravagant experience, like when a woman poured a bottle of perfume on Jesus before he went to the cross (John 12:1-8). Although the sisters and most of the guests contrived not to enjoy or speak of it, the meal was sacramental, lifting them beyond their mundane lives and rekindling a sense of sacredness and forgotten love. We learn from such acts of shalom the value of hospitality and the importance of helping people enjoy their everyday life to the full.

Hebrew Wholeness and Monastic Rhythms

Read the Bible through a missionary lens, and it quickly becomes apparent that God's dream is the restoration of all things. And so restoration is a central aspect of the work of God's sent people. In contrast to a consumer culture, which is oriented toward the individual and gives little sustained thought to relationship or the needs of others, God's missionary people seek restoration for individuals and communities—reconciled relationships, mutually supportive networks of people, environmental and social responsibility, and a vision for peace and flourishing under God.

Shalom is an ancient Hebrew concept of wholeness, well-being, delight and completeness. It can be translated as "peace," but it is much more than the absence of conflict; it is the presence and fullness of welfare and peace between people or nations, or between people and God. It is often used as a greeting or sung as a benediction: "Shalom, my friends, God's peace, my friends, be with you now." But it conveys much more than a casual hello or goodbye; it is an expression of hope for everyone to have all that is best. Cornelius Plantinga describes it holistically:

> In the Bible, shalom means *universal flourishing, wholeness and delight*—a rich state of affairs in which natural needs are sat-

isfied and natural gifts fruitfully employed, a state of affairs that inspires joyful wonder as its Creator and Savior opens doors and welcomes the creatures in whom he delights. Shalom, in other words, is the way things ought to be.[1]

Shalom is good news to a world wracked by conflict and hungry for authentic spirituality. It evokes a world entirely under God's direction and care. God invites us to experience shalom and share it in the world. Shalom spirituality embraces all of life under Jesus as the Messiah.[2] Alan Hirsch considers the phrase "Jesus is Lord" the foundational element of the missional DNA of the church: "Our task is to make *all* aspects and dimensions of life sacred—family, work, play, conflict, etc.—and not to limit the presence of God to spooky religious zones."[3]

Shalom, then, is not a spirituality of worship and devotion on Sundays. It is a spirituality of everyday life. A shalom spirituality discourages navel-gazing, private, individual spiritual practices limited to Sunday temple events. It does not extract people from their world, but encourages us to engage our "worldly" responsibilities with attentiveness to God's purposes for the world. It helps us live for the Messiah seven days a week.

Roger Helland and Leonard Hjalmarson see shalom spirituality as a mixture of inner spiritual resources and a commitment to engaging the world: "The task of God's people . . . is to be at home with God (in spirituality) as they also serve [God's] agenda in the world (in mission)."[4]

Without exception, all the followers of Jesus we know are trying to bring shalom with them wherever they go, no matter how broken the city, neighborhood or situation is. These are the people you want cutting the red wire at a bomb site. They seek and facilitate reconciliation everywhere they go. Whether they work in a war zone or a racially conflicted inner city, they carry the peace of the Holy Spirit in the midst of turmoil. Where do they get this overflowing well of love and joy? They practice spiritual direction; they pray regularly; they read new and ancient texts; and they wait and are still in the midst of ever-increasing busyness and danger. They regularly practice ancient ways as they seek to bring good news to all.

More to Spirituality Than a Quiet Time?

We love to ask people when they feel closest to God. It is a fallacy that what works for me is something you should do. We are thankful that no one has to fit anyone else's spirituality mold.

It is helpful to remind ourselves that people in our communities draw close to God in different ways. For some Christians, spirituality centers on prayer and Bible reading in a "quiet time" each day. These can be very helpful practices. We grew up on them. I (Darren) am thankful my family took me to church and gave me Scripture Union and Every Day with Jesus booklets to guide me in Bible reading. In some seasons the Bible has been as easy to read as the latest John Grisham novel. God feels close, and quiet times are as regular as breakfast. At other times, it has been a harder discipline—when the Bible seems dry and God seems distant. But the habit of engaging with the Bible each day, or most days, has given me regular space to reconnect with God.

For me (Kim), spirituality revolved around church and Christian school, with a basic foundation of love for God that came from home. Spirituality was prayer on my own or in prayer meetings, preferably with lots of singing. These were the first spiritual practices that helped me cultivate prayer and openness to God's Word.

In college and afterward, we both discovered different devotional practices and ancient traditions that helped broaden and deepen our spirituality. We practiced quietness and silence for centering our souls, fasting for focusing our minds and prayer, and *lectio divina*—slow, contemplative reading of the Bible. My (Darren) spiritual director told me I could use gardening and walking as spiritual exercises. After one session, she sent me home to go outside and nurture my fruit trees; on the next available sabbath I was to go up to the mountains for a coffee, walk and mutual spiritual direction retreat with my wife, Jenni. We love conversation, activity, engaging culture and enjoying creation—all as part of a wholesome spirituality. Our souls are glad that we can cultivate spirituality through walks as well as Bible study, conversation as well as contemplation, fruit trees as well as fasting and movies as well as meditation.

I (Kim) need to get away and pray, to get up early or stay up late (more often late than early). I need to read my Bible and get lost in the Word and the words of Jesus as if nothing else matters. In that meditation I focus on the unseen things—the supernatural things. I slow down enough to know God cares about my soul. I get lost in worship. I don't care about the worship style; it's focusing on God that helps my confession and communion with him.

But some of the best news for our spirituality has come from another direction. We have discovered we can also engage God in the midst of action and community life.

We certainly understand that slowing down and practicing quiet contemplation is a helpful corrective to modern workaholic and driven tendencies. As activists we need silence and solitude for balance. We have rediscovered sabbath as a regular time to slow down and remind ourselves that the work does not revolve around us. These are growing edges for our walks with God and essential for long-term sustainability. But we also celebrate that God can speak to us and be with us as we are and in the midst of conversation and action. God is not removed from our reading, sports, movies or friends. And God is not disengaged from our mission and our work for shalom in the world. Quiet, introverted spirituality is not the only way to experience God. "Hallelujah!" says our extroverted souls.[5]

We reckon spirituality is expressed in seeking shalom for ourselves but also for the world around us. It is something we cultivate on the road and not just in our quiet times. A shalom spirituality is life giving for the world and for us because it integrates active engagement with contemplative retreat. It is ministry as well as a retreat, relationships as well as soul work, loud advocacy as well as quiet prayer. It worships outdoors in the forest as well as indoors in the chapel.

There is a cycle of missional action and missional reflection that is intrinsic to missional spirituality. Ross Langmead practiced and taught a "theological reflection for mission" that encourages grassroots engagement with places that need shalom, but also maintains space for fostering reflection on where we are in our practice of mission and spirituality. As a person of good news, he realized that mission drew him to difficult areas that needed transformation, but he warned,

> If mission were all action, with no reflection, we would go off the rails. We would "hard sell" the gospel, organize our way to being an international brand name, manage the church and cram every living moment with mission activity. But it's mission with mystery, and waiting is as important as outreach, listening as speaking, responding as pro-active planning. The reflective and meditative dimension of mission is central.[6]

Ross was committed to action and advocacy for people in need, and in his songwriting and prayer he was committed to making space for reflection—all to feed back into ongoing mission.[7] Contemplation is never an elective on top of mission but an essential basis and inspiration for how we practice mission.

LEARNING ON THE ROAD

We love that Jesus seems to have always had in mind team building and leadership development for mission. He shared life with the

disciples and modeled for them what it meant to foster the kingdom
of God and minister peace and healing, and then he sent them out
in pairs to do it. We are thankful that God does not call us to
mission on our own, but places us with other people. We do not
always choose whom God puts us with. Some of the disciples might
not have chosen to go out with the partner Jesus sent them with
either. But Jesus knows what he is doing when he puts us in teams.
Like Gimli and Legolas in the Lord of the Rings, we sometimes
grow closest to and learn the most from people who are very different from us.

One story that captures our imagination and that is enthusing
many missional churches globally is the sending of the seventy-two
disciples. This passage in Luke 10 is kind of like a postmodern
Great Commission and a helpful model for mission to the West. It
shows the disciples learning on the road.

Luke 10 begins with a call to prayer. As in Jesus' time, we face a
huge harvest and need. Kim's boss at Community Christian Church,
Dave Ferguson, likes to say that if the world were a village of one
hundred people, twenty would live in extreme poverty and sixty-
seven would live far from God. We need to focus our mission and
prayer on the twenty and the sixty-seven.[8] That's why Jesus asked
his followers to pray for more laborers (Luke 10:2). One simple way
to do this is to set an alarm and pray for more missional leaders
every morning at 10:02 a.m.

Jesus sent these first missionaries with some counterintuitive
instructions. He told them not to take an extra purse, bag or sandals
and not to greet anyone on the road (Luke 10:4). We suspect Jesus
wanted his followers to rely on the hospitality of the people in the
towns where they were going. He wanted them not just to be sent
but to submerge.

Then he said to find a place to stay and bless it with "Peace be on
this house." They were to stay there, not moving around from house

to house (vv. 5-7). Stability rather than mobility was to be the norm.

The larger context of Jesus' ministry with the disciples, of course, was itinerant. And after the resurrection, diaspora was more the norm than stability. The disciples witnessed in Jerusalem and Judea but also in Samaria and to the ends of the known world (Acts 1:8). But we are learning that sentness is not itinerancy for its own sake. The happy wayfarer is not the ideal model for mission. The model for mission is seeking the welfare of a place. Somehow shalom encompasses staying and being sent.

There was a time when monks were free to go from monastery to monastery. If the worship was not exciting or the abbot was too bossy or the bed was too hard, a monk might pack up his few belongings and go looking for a better place down the road. Saint Benedict saw that this was not good for the monastic cause (or for the monk's soul), so he laid down a new requirement for aspiring monks coming to his monastery: a vow of stability. Basically, you say, "No matter what problems I face, I am ready to stay here and work through how to serve God in this place."

Benedict's vow of stability was a prophetic critique of the tendency to treat rootlessness as a sign of piety. But you don't just go; you go where you're sent, and there you stay until you're sent elsewhere. New monastics and others today are helping us see that "staying is the new going" and that for the sake of fruitfulness, stability rather than mobility needs to be our norm.[9] (When I [Darren] told my wife, Jenni, about this after we'd moved eighteen times in fifteen years, she asked, "Where do I sign?")

Stability was a challenge for God's people in Jeremiah's day. Israel had been carried off in exile to Babylon. They could not worship in the temple, because it had been destroyed, and they were far from Jerusalem—the place where they thought God and their destiny lay. Their whole sense of faith had been turned on its head. It was a disaster. They did not know what God was doing.

God's word for the exiles was stability:

> Build homes, and plan to stay. Plant gardens, and eat the food
> they produce. Marry and have children. Then find spouses for
> them so that you may have many grandchildren. Multiply! Do
> not dwindle away! And work for the peace and prosperity of
> the city where I sent you into exile. Pray to the LORD for it, for
> its welfare will determine your welfare. (Jeremiah 29:5-7)

This was Babylon—the most depraved place, where the people worshiped all sorts of other gods. Jeremiah was encouraging the Israelite exiles to make their homes there, rather than long to be somewhere else, and to seek its peace and prosperity. God told them not to expect escape from there any time soon, but to pray for the city, plan to be there for decades and put roots down. In that context Jeremiah spoke these words of hope: "'For I know the plans I have for you,' says the LORD. 'They are plans for good and not for disaster, to give you a future and a hope. In those days when you pray, I will listen. If you look for me wholeheartedly, you will find me'" (Jeremiah 29:11-13).

In the place where they thought God was completely absent and where he had left them alone, God invited them to encounter him afresh and to be a channel of blessing to their city. God often calls people to go somewhere new—and we need to be open to that. But God also often invites us to stay—and we need to be open to that countercultural adventure too.

RESENDING A MISSIONARY DROPOUT

Fifteen years ago I (Darren) thought our mission organization, Global Interaction, was sending us to the ends of the earth; instead we ended up back in Melbourne. We had been preparing for mission overseas for ten years, been candidates with the mission for three years and were sent to Indonesia with the ideal of serving for seven to seventeen years. But we returned to Melbourne after eight months and never got back long term.

To say there was disappointment involved would be an understatement. We had joined the missionary dropout statistics. Global Interaction was fantastic in caring for us, helping us sort through our options and—when it became obvious we could not get back to Indonesia—helping us resettle in Australia. But there were vocational, faith, health and marriage crises involved. I had been sure God had called us overseas, but when things did not work out my heart wondered how we could seek and trust God's guidance again. My Bible reading seemed dry. It felt like my prayers were bouncing off the ceiling.

With the help of some friends and with some spiritual direction, I learned several important lessons. First, I learned to love God independent of whatever mission I was involved in. Second, I learned to love my family independent of their capacity to follow me to the ends of the earth. And third, I learned that mission does not start by getting onto a plane. What seemed like a vocational closed door turned into new opportunities for mission and training in another direction—staying at home. I am convinced now that the Jesus we follow, who called and sent us overseas on mission, also calls and sends us to stay where we are here.

Jenni and I came to Auburn with a ministry plan for a decade or more. In the eighteen times we had moved in fifteen years, we had served in interim pastoral roles, a short term overseas and some housesitting while we worked out what we were doing. The longest we had stayed in one suburb was three years. We longed to put our roots down and foster shalom for a local community where we could stay. I read about pastor Eugene Peterson's desire to get to know his parish block, and then to keep getting to know it.[10] I realized that local mission and deep cultural engagement take time.

Now we are in a church that is neighbors and tenants with Global

Interaction. It is a church community I am thankful for every day. But it is interesting for me that I serve as a pastor in inner-suburban Melbourne, in a church with the central offices of the mission organization that sent us to Indonesia. And there is no place I would rather be sent to stay than here, where God has sent me.

UNSHOCKABLE

Alongside Jesus' challenge to stay, a related instruction was to "eat whatever is set before you" (Luke 10:8). That is more of a challenge in some kitchens than others. We have been in Asian countries where interesting foods were served, and we had to gather up the courage to eat so as not to offend our host. I (Darren) recall a beautiful spread of potluck dishes after church one Sunday in Indonesia. The proud host shared his very own "hot dog" culinary creation with me, but it did not look or taste like the meat in a bun I would expect at a baseball game.

Eating "what is set before you" challenges us to engage in whatever conversation, books and ideas people in our neighborhoods want to talk about. There are still Bibles and occasional books by evangelical writers in general bookstores. But usually there is only one shelf or bookcase set aside for these Christian books—and often it is at the back of the store. Have you noticed what books are most popular? The number of books on topics like cooking, home improvement, sexuality and relationships shows that people are very interested in these sides of life. We are amazed at the number of self-help and do-it-yourself spirituality books, which must be selling in high volume.

We discipline ourselves to take an interest in the books people are reading. Have a look at the books on people's shelves, or ask them what they are reading. Keep your eye on what is popular in local bookstores. We have had valuable conversations with people about all kinds of books with implications for faith and spirituality—from *The Celestine Prophecy* to *The Da Vinci Code*, from books by popular but controversial theologians to J. K. Rowling's Harry Potter series.

We are also careful to be unshockable in conversation. Shock can inhibit the pursuit of shalom. There are things our neighbors are engaged in that we might not agree with. But we do not feel we always have to stand up for what is righteous and tell people that what they are reading or eating or drinking or doing is wrong. When friends say to us, "I don't know how you can believe in God" or "Last weekend we enjoyed visiting Sexpo" or "Did you see the last episode of *Desperate Housewives?*" we explore what their comments reflect. Let's engage in conversations rather than prudishly avoid talking about alternative spirituality, sexuality or soaps.

Sent people are sent to stay but also sent to heal—not to turn away from those who are different from us. We can minister healing and wholeness in all sorts of ways, including the emotional support of a listening ear and companionship through life's struggles. The example of Jesus and his disciples in the Gospels also urges us to offer to pray for miraculous healing and to invite God to demonstrate his love and power tangibly. Whether or not miraculous healing happens, and whether or not people received the message, the final word now is the same as then: "The Kingdom of God is near" (Luke 10:9-11).

In Luke 10, when the disciples came back to Jesus, they were excited that the demons submitted to them (v. 17). They had a story to celebrate—a dangerous story. They had been able to share a whole vision of shalom—a reality of shalom—with their adopted neighborhoods.[11] What did shalom mean for the villages the disciples visited? It meant healing and deliverance, peace and hospitality, and a reorientation of community life to the way things ought to be, in line with God's dream for the world.

MORE THAN HEAVEN EVER AFTER

Andrew Knight, writer of the popular Australian television series *SeaChange*, spoke at a World Vision event saying he loved supporting World Vision but did not understand the Christian bit. Tim Costello, a Baptist minister and World Vision's Australian CEO, asked him what bit, and he replied, "Heaven."

Floating on clouds, playing a harp and daily Bible study did not offer significant doses of hope to Knight. He suggested, cheekily, "You really need to do better than that—at least the Muslims seem to offer virgins in the afterlife."[12]

Ironically, Knight is in sync with one of the most significant theological rediscoveries of recent times. The church is realizing that salvation is not just about saving souls for eternity but also about restoring God's dream and shalom for our current world. This realignment comes when we understand the nature of the kingdom of God.

When Jesus came and ministered on earth, he set people free of bondage, healed people of their illnesses and even raised people from the dead. His ministry was about restoring people to the ideal of what God had created them for—the completeness and welfare of shalom. When Jesus did this for people, he said, "The Kingdom of God has arrived" (Matthew 12:28). The kingdom of God can be understood as where God's dream for the world is brought to reality. *Missio Dei*, then, is fostering the kingdom of God, the dream of God or the shalom of God. It is not just about getting as many souls as possible across the line into heaven and rescuing them from a bad world, but redeeming and restoring the world and inviting people to work with God toward that dream of shalom.

N. T. Wright is a scholar whose theology of hope is not just about heaven but also about remaking our world, for now and afterward. He challenges Christians to own their citizenship in heaven proudly (Philippians 3:20-21), but also to colonize and transform the earth. Jesus was crucified, he reminds us, not just so our personal sins could be forgiven, but also to overcome the evil that enslaves the world and to restore the world to God's ideal. The kingdom of God is not something we have to wait for heaven to see realized, but has begun here on earth. It is manifest in the life, death and resurrection of Jesus and through the Spirit-led work of the church.[13]

A kingdom-of-God perspective has huge implications for how we see mission and spirituality. It helps remind us that mission is far broader than just evangelism. It includes acts of compassion and advocacy for justice, care for creation and inclusive hospitality. But mission still must include verbally communicating what really is good news about Jesus and inviting people to respond. The challenge is moving beyond a narrow set of ideas about heaven and hell. God is intimately interested in what happens here on earth for all people, not just what will happen one day in heaven for God's chosen people.

At Forge we do not avoid tackling the big issues of our day. For example, we proudly celebrate the contribution and leadership of women. And we are committed to praying and working for restoration of ethnic equality and advocating that we learn from one another. We advocate for environmental care and restoration of the earth. And we advocate against injustices wherever we see them, including the trafficking of women and children. God planted us in particular places at this time in history and wants to work through us to bring shalom into our contexts. The kingdom of God is more than heaven ever after; it includes bringing heaven to earth.

WILL'S NEIGHBORS

Will is married with two children, and they have lived in their neighborhood for four years. For their first two years there, Will and his family hardly knew the people that lived around them. Most of their time and energy was spent with people they already knew and went to church with. Will began to sense that he was missing something in his faith. He realized that he had been neglecting the very thing that God had called him to: to live as salt to the unsalty, as light in the darkness, as a sent one and a missionary. He was sent to bring heaven to earth.

As Will and his family prayed about the implications of this, Will realized that he had to apologize to his neighbors for neglecting the relationships that had been right under his nose. His family began to see all their neighbors as people of value, people who could bring value to their own lives—even though the neighbors did not believe the same things they did about God and Jesus. Will and his family began to spend regular and consistent time with their neighbors, asking, "What is the gospel, and what is good news to the people we live among?"

As they developed a friendship with one family on their street, they learned that the husband and wife had a rocky marriage. They both worked long days, and they had two children with extracurricular activities, leaving little time for them to be together and work on their relationship. Will and his wife began to realize that this husband and wife had not been out on a date in a long time; good news for them might be a night out to talk and connect. So Will and his family offered to watch their children one Friday night for free while they went out.

Will and his family are embodying shalom spirituality in this act of kindness. They are demonstrating a piece of the gospel and have given their neighbors hope for a redeemed and whole marriage. Will and his family continue to deepen their relationship with this family, and the Lord has allowed them opportunities both to demonstrate and to proclaim what the gospel is about.

MONASTIC RHYTHMS

In advocating shalom spirituality, we want to hold mission and spirituality together. They belong together. To be fruitful and sustainable in mission, we need spiritual foundations. But to exercise authentic spirituality, we need to have a missional outlet and be active with our faith.

We can learn about this helpful rhythm of mission and spirituality from the monastic tradition. Monasticism was never just about withdrawing, but integrating inner life with outward service. Saint Francis of Assisi, a hero of ours, had a healthy rhythm of engaging fully with people and their struggles on the margins of society and regularly retreating to the wilderness to encounter God, creation and himself. He sought not just a prayer life but a whole life of prayer.[14]

Thomas Merton, a Trappist monk from the twentieth century, wrote that a monk "abandons the world only in order to listen more intently to the deepest and most neglected voices that proceed from its inner depth."[15] Combining and integrating contemplation and action is intrinsic to monasticism. According to Richard Rohr, founder of the Center for Action and Contemplation, the most important word in his center's name is *and*: "'And' demands that our contemplation become action; 'And' insists that our action is also contemplative."[16] As we imagine a church with an identity of sentness and equipped to foster shalom, we realize we need this rhythm of contemplation and action.

In the busyness of everyday life and mission, it is crucial for us to pause regularly for solitude so we can ponder where God is working. Attentiveness and contemplation are gifts to help us understand the world and ourselves, and to expand our idea of God. We can be contemplative and attentive in our private prayer, and even when we are reading or studying and when we are active in mission or in conversation with people. We love how Simone Weil applies a prayerful approach to study: "It is the orientation of all the attention of which the soul is capable toward God."[17]

We have learned and practiced different devotional practices at different seasons of our lives to help nurture contemplation and

attentiveness. Prayer, worship, gratitude, Bible memorization, jour-
naling, spiritual warfare and prayer walking are some of the practices we first learned and are still growing in. We have tried and
appreciated fasting, centering prayer, silent retreats and liturgy.
Sabbath is probably one of the best disciplines for helping us slow
down and reminding us that the world does not revolve around us.
Silence, solitude and slowness are a stretch for us, so they are good
to return to and to practice regularly.

Our hero of a pastor and contemplative guru is Eugene Peterson.
His books on pastoral ministry, everyday spirituality, discipleship
and parenting are among our favorites. He champions a contemplative approach to ministry with three practices or angles that
shape pastoral integrity:

- Prayer brings us to attention before God.

- Scripture focuses our attention on God's speech and actions in
  the history of Israel and the church.

- Spiritual direction gives attention to what God is doing in a
  person.[18]

Now, here is a radical thought: Peterson argues that effective
mission begins in attentiveness to God.

> Anything creative, anything powerful, anything *biblical*, in-
> sofar as we are participants in it, originates in prayer. Pastors
> who imitate the preaching and moral action of the prophets
> without also imitating the prophets' deep praying and worship
> so evident in the Psalms are an embarrassment to the faith and
> an encumbrance to the church.[19]

Prayer, Scripture and spiritual direction help shape the agenda
of our work as pastors, but they equally shape the wholeness of
shalom spirituality for all of God's people. These are not novel or
new ideas. But as we experiment with innovative ideas in how we

express the life of our churches, we never want to leave behind these life sources.

ENGAGED SPIRITUALITY

What we describe as shalom spirituality, which is really just biblical spirituality or authentic spirituality as practiced by the saints throughout history, is not quiet contemplation without active engagement. It goes outward in serving the world and inward in drawing close to God. An outer move of engagement needs an inner move of contemplation to be sustainable. Yet contemplative prayer needs missional engagement to be complete—to express shalom in its fullness.

Alan Hirsch and Mike Frost suggest that missional engagement is the best context for contemplation: "One worships more fully, prays more deeply, and studies more diligently when all are done in the context of a life of action."[20] Embracing our sentness and moving beyond consumer Christianity require this integration of contemplation and missional engagement:

> Too much Christendom spirituality has been concerned with retreat and reflection. While we acknowledge the value of a rich interior life, as well as the value of solitude in interiority, we believe that retreat and reflection should be embraced as part of a broader spirituality that values engagement and action. We need to find a renewed framework and basis for understanding everyday life and our actions as a vital source of experience of God. We believe in the need for the recovery of a *messianic* spirituality, one rooted primarily in the life and teaching of Jesus himself.[21]

Jesus modeled a spirituality of contemplation and engagement, often teaching, healing and eating with all sorts of people, but he also retreated to pray and to seek guidance in solitary places.

Alongside more interior spiritual practices, we foster shalom spirituality through *outer* spiritual practices of neighborliness, exercise,
sports, witnessing, interfaith dialogue, social action, hiking, pil-
grimage, generosity, friendship, dancing, hospitality and incarnational presence in community networks and online conversations.
These practices help us engage with and cooperate with God and
reflect God's love of life and of people. They are platforms to celebrate and foster shalom, and they help inform our more focused
times of prayer and contemplative practices.

Romans 12 captures this for us, and we especially like *The
Message* paraphrase of verses 1-2: "So here's what I want you to do,
God helping you: Take your everyday, ordinary life—your sleeping,
eating, going-to-work, and walking-around life—and place it before
God as an offering. Embracing what God does for you is the best
thing you can do for him." True spirituality is not just about offering God one hour or five minutes of our day for a read-and-pray
(with an extra couple of hours on Sunday for a sing and a listen),
but offering God all of our days to foster shalom in the world.

Shalom spirituality, as an aspect of missional imagination, looks
for how God connects with our cultural contexts, as well as what
aspects of our culture and community need redemption. Roger
Helland and Leonard Hjalmarson critique any spirituality located
in the "monastery apart from the marketplace." A missional church,
they suggest, needs to know and exegete Oprah, *Lost* and Lady
Gaga as well as Hillsong and James Dobson. It is important to view
films like *Chocolat*, *Voyage of the Dawn Treader* and *Lars and the Real
Girl* as well as to consult Bible commentaries. We also need theological reflection on cultural obsessions—fitness and home renova-
tions, reality TV and online dating, catering and holidays, consumerism and self-improvement, and so on.[22] These are places where
people are looking for significance and meaning.

EASTERN HILLS'S REFLECTION OF KINGDOM LIFE

Toliu and Emma Morgan and a group of young adults from Temple-
stowe Baptist imagined a shift to a new kind of church that would
engage with the world's challenges and popular culture.[23] They
talked about getting a fresh picture of Jesus and then shaping
mission and church. In 2002 they met as a dreaming group and
discussed N. T. Wright's books about Jesus. Toli and his fellow
budding scholars had their imaginations captured by Jesus' decla-
ration that the kingdom of God is not just about inner peace of
mind or a heaven after the current space-time continuum, and by
the story of God becoming king and putting the world right.[24]

One member of the group, Krystal, saw the "real Jesus" with new
eyes as someone who "knows what is going on in the world and . . .
is willing to have a heart and compassion and love for all the world."
This understanding of Jesus had implications for her contemporary
context: "What happens over in a factory over in China, really af-
fects us."[25]

The picture of Jesus that inspired Toliu and the others led them
to plant Eastern Hills Community Church. Their vision, "creating
lives which reflect the kingdom of God," has led to a range of missional initiatives. They started a soup kitchen, a high school ministry, movie-making nights and a soccer competition for African
youth. They have taught English to refugees and helped struggling
families with education and housing access. They have plans to
develop some form of cohousing, building houses for themselves
and for refugees and others in need of rental accommodation.

Eastern Hills takes a broad interest in social justice. They sell
fair-trade goods and compiled a "Sunday best" cookbook for a con-
servation charity. Their engagement with the world arises out of
their desire to help make it more like the kingdom of God. One
morning when Darren visited, they sang "Lord, Have Your Way,"
and invited people to voice concerns. People mentioned problems

in Uganda, indigenous communities, people coming out of slavery, Iran, Iraq, East Timor, Jakarta, "my classroom," Croydon Secondary School, mercy and wisdom for world leaders, people in prison (especially a particular friend) and people in local Supported Residential Services housing. After praying for these concerns—mostly for people on the margins and for troubled regions of the world—the worship leader prayed in a kind of "by the way, God" prayer for "our families and those not with us today." Their commitment to pray for shalom for the world was a refreshing contrast to pastoral prayer times where a congregation focuses on themselves and their friends and family, and the worship leader's "by the way" prayer is for the broader world.

Eastern Hills holds a strong conviction about their spirituality and worship empowering them for mission. "We believe the Holy Spirit sends us to our homes, local community and wider world and empowers us to bring about love, truth, hope, healing, beauty and justice." Sunday input often involves the vocations and everyday experiences of participants. One Sunday "prayer journey" offered prayer stations with music CDs and kitchen utensils, children's books and diapers, sports gear, books and newspapers. The congregation was invited to wander among the stations, contemplating how God is involved in the various aspects of our lives represented in these diverse items. After twenty minutes, participants were asked to write down the people and places they would encounter that week. The papers were swapped so they could pray for one another's "spaces and faces." This was a thoughtful exercise to help people be prayerfully aware of where the church was bringing life and shalom through the week.

The purpose of any spiritual exercise—contemplative or engaged—is to help the character and person of Christ be formed in us. Naturally, if we become more like Christ we adopt his servanthood and mission heart. Any authentic Christian spirituality will be missional and foster shalom. Robert Mulholland Jr. describes spiritual formation as "a process of being conformed to the image of Christ *for the sake of others.*"[26] Robert Webber says, "Spirituality is our mystical union with God through Jesus by the Spirit that results in our participation in the life of the Triune God *in the life of the world.*"[27]

We are invited into the dance of God. God sends the people of God into the world, but he is also already active in the world and invites us to join with God moving, creating and dancing in the world. Spirituality prepares us for that. Those of us who are activists need the foundation of a vibrant spirituality; those who are contemplatives need the outlet of world-engaging mission. This is the dance that shalom spirituality invites us into—following Jesus and participating with God in his mission in the world.

5

SAFE PLACES

I myself will tend my sheep and have them lie down, declares the
*Sovereign L*ORD*. I will search for the lost and bring back the strays.*
I will bind up the injured and strengthen the weak.

E*ZEKIEL* **34:15-16** (NIV)

Is it not more fitting that we adopt the attitude
of a humble seeker after truth, keeping an open mind,
ready to listen to all that comes from the varied religious experience
of the human race? Is it not more honest as well as more humble
to stop preaching and engage rather in dialogue, listening to
the experience of others and offering our own?

L*ESSLIE* N*EWBIGIN*

LEPROSY **IS A HORRIBLE DISEASE.** During Jesus' time, people
who caught it were marginalized and forced to leave their family
and friends. Looked down on and rejected, they had to live in iso-

lation. Imagine this in a rural society where everyone knows everyone else. If you catch leprosy, you hide away. When your eyes lock with others, they recoil in fear. See old friends in the street, and they cross the street to avoid you. You are obligated—in fact, commanded—to call out, "Unclean!" if someone inadvertently comes too close. Your friends and your family can no longer see you, hug you or interact with you in any way. In fact, rabbis had to keep a hundred feet between them and anyone who may be unclean. Some women, the poor and the infirm were all unclean, but lepers were considered especially unclean. They could not go to the temple for worship or the market to buy goods or work or eat with anyone. On top of that, people assumed that lepers had upset God in some terrible way. So lepers were truly on the outer margins of society. Imagine what that would do for your self-esteem.

Jesus was a Jewish rabbi, so people did not expect he would have anything to do with a leper. But when a leper came begging to him, and said, "If you are willing, you can heal me and make me clean" (Mark 1:40)—a statement of faith as well as a plea—Jesus was moved with pity—and perhaps with anger at the injustice that lepers experienced on a regular basis. He responded, "I am willing." Then he commanded, "Be healed!"

The leprosy disappeared, and the man was healed. He had his physical wellness restored to him, but also his community. His community could once again be a safe place for him to go.

Jesus urged him to go quietly and show the priest he was healed, but the man told everyone he saw about what had become good news for him: He was safe! He was home!

Do you create safe places for those who need it? Do you advocate for those who don't have a voice? For some churches, this is as simple as realizing that the needs of young people are vastly different from those of other generations. For other churches, the growing edge is inviting and welcoming the voices of culturally diverse backgrounds. We want to welcome people of different cultures not just into our churches but into our worship, onto our mission teams and as valuable members on our leadership and pastoral teams. Prejudice plays against the church being all it can be. Jesus invites all different sorts of people to be valued parts and contributors in his church.

A friend of ours came to Forge in Melbourne a few years ago. Debra Hirsch, one of Forge's cofounders, had counseled her over the years, and she had been part of Deb's church. She had been born a boy but did not feel she could live as a boy, so now she lives as a girl. Early in her transition, she was counseled by a church to repent. This had a very negative effect on her, but she kept feeling drawn back; she wanted to belong and to express her faith in Jesus.

Because she was not going to fit or be accepted in many traditional churches, Deb and I (Darren) started a group with her and some housemates called Body & Soul. When Deb moved to the States, our friend joined me and my family and some others in forming a neighborhood church experiment called Bimbadeen Tribe. We followed Michael Frost's outline for church life and for home-group gatherings called BELLS: Bless one another, Eat together, Learn about Jesus, Listen to one another and Send into mission. We laughed and wept together as we shared our faith stories, meals, prayer and discussions about Jesus. The group met together for eighteen months. Journeying together and hearing about our friend's struggles with relationships and sexuality led us to ask how we do church in ways that are safe for people on a journey like hers.[1]

OFFERING SAFE SPACE

Jon Owen, a missionary in Sydney with Urban Neighbours of Hope (UNOH), tells the story of two families—neighbors that had been arguing and facing each other off. The police needed to be called regularly, and at one point two police officers were stationed in a car on the block for an entire week on the expectation that one particular argument would soon escalate to violence. The two police officers proved not to be enough, however, as the fight spread to include a hundred people.

The fight made headlines in the media. Questions were asked. People wanted to blame someone. The most striking commentary was from a community police officer, who matter-of-factly said,

> As the tension was bubbling away before the riot, all it would have taken was for one respected, non-partisan member of the local community to stand up and say "Enough is enough, Let's talk" and it would have been enough to have gotten both sides to communicate, and yet, there was no one, no one willing to take a stand for the local neighborhood. All it needed was one person, and that person did not step forward.[2]

We are learning that part of the danger of Jesus' call is found in being involved in restoring the world from situations that bring tears to our eyes and that break the heart of God. Who of us is willing to count the cost and create safe places when our neighborhoods are distant from God's dream and needing restoration?

Early one morning in Jerusalem, Jesus was teaching at the temple. Early mornings were busy times in the streets. People were setting up market booths, preparing for work, listening to the latest news.

This morning, a bunch of rowdy-looking men—actually religious leaders—dragged a woman into the scene. Jesus already had a crowd around him. Now the numbers swelled with scribes and Pharisees. Claiming they had caught the woman in the act of adultery, they dragged her in to set up a test for Jesus. He hangs out with sinners, so what will he say about this sinner? He preaches grace and forgiveness, but how can he extend that to her?

"Teacher," they said, "the law says she should be stoned. What do you reckon?" They were not honestly curious about his wisdom but were baiting him. They were using the woman as an object lesson to score religious points.

People leaned forward to hear Jesus' response. Others gathered as they heard that controversy was imminent and violence likely. The most self-righteous pointed to the woman with disdain. They sniggered at Jesus, wondering how his disciples thought he would get out of this one.

"So what do you say, Jesus?" they asked. The question hung in the air. It was an early version of "What would Jesus do?" except it was not asked with the intention of imitation but to trap him.

The religious leaders were confident they would come out on top. Either Jesus would affirm what they believed and assure them they were better than this woman, or they would have evidence that Jesus was not keeping the religious rules about how people express their sexuality.

As Jon Owen comments, these religious leaders were playing the enemy-making game that works so well: saying this person or type of person is the cause of our moral decay.[3] Condemnatory preachers and conniving politicians know this strategy. Pick a vulnerable group, use them as a scapegoat, play on fears of invasion or terrorism or financial loss, and you can get the mob on your side. "Watch out, the communists are coming." "Homosexuals are the cause of all the moral problems in society." "Indigenous and First Nations people are only after money." The target changes but the message of fear is the same.

Jesus was given the platform to respond. But to the frustration of the religious leaders, he said nothing in reply. Instead he bent down and scribbled in the dirt. There are plenty of theories about what he wrote—perhaps a Bible verse or the judgment before he announced it or the names of the men's girlfriends. Maybe he doodled Xs and Os to pass the time. Perhaps he wrote nothing at all. Whatever he scribbled, he refused to be drawn into the escalating violence.

Have you ever been in an argument and said something that inflamed the situation? At times it's better to be silent. And Jesus knows some questions are not worth answering. They're not worth the breath. They're not worth getting drawn in.

But they push him. So Jesus stands up and says, "All right, go ahead and stone the woman, right here in front of us all."

Some men juggle their rocks at the ready. The crowd goes silent. That's not quite what they expected.

"Let's do this in the right order though," Jesus adds.

"You'll all get your turn," he says in his best schoolmaster voice. "How about we line up? Those of you who have never sinned, at the front of the line, and the rest of you behind. . . . Let them who are without sin among you be the first to throw a stone."

And then Jesus goes back to his doodling, having dared those who think they are completely righteous to stone her.

Jesus was not setting himself up as a great debater or politician. A master at reconciliation and community peacemaking, he tackled the real issue—not whether the woman should be stoned, but how the religious leaders thought they had the right to condemn her to death. Jesus did not condemn the woman but confronted the group—the socioreligious system—that opposed respect for people, that questioned the value of life and that threatened justice. That gave them something to think about.

The silence was broken only by the sound of rocks dropping with a thud onto the ground and the sandaled feet of everyone— first the wisest elders and then the rest—walking away. Why? Because Jesus had made a safe place for her. Jesus does that, and we love him for it.

Jesus placed himself between the woman and the crowd. If the stones had started flying, he would have been in the line of fire. Jesus was ready to be stoned alongside a woman labeled as a sexual sinner. Jesus does that. And we love that about him.

Jesus makes a safe place for us when we struggle with falling short of God's expectations, when we become aware of our sin and our lack of desire to live God's ways, when we struggle with lack of purpose and meaning, when other people or our own self-talk say to us, "You're not worth it. You're not going to get better" or "How could you do that?! You may as well give up." Jesus is there, standing in the gap, making a safe place, not just once but again and again— for us and for you. Jesus does that, and we love him for it.

After the crowd disperses, Jesus looks up from his doodling and talks with the woman for the first time. "Dear woman, where are they? Is no one pointing their finger at you anymore? Have they gone?" It looks that way. "Neither do I condemn you." She stands there forgiven, free, liberated. It's as if something too good to be true has happened. Jesus does that, and we love that about him.

Jesus has not finished though. He straightens up, looks at her and gives her a fresh focus for living: "Go, and from now on, don't sin anymore." Jesus is not into the sloppy acceptance of anything goes, as if there were no boundaries on human behavior. He doesn't condemn the woman, but still has her well-being in mind when he challenges her to a higher life and calling. Part of affirming this woman is standing in the gap for her and saying boldly, "No, that is not the way to treat her." And part of it is saying kindly, "No, that is not the way to live anymore." She receives mercy for what others might condemn her for. And she receives hope for the future that others did not want to offer her. Jesus does that, and we love and follow him for it.

Tim Winton's Neighbors

Tim Winton is one of Australia's most popular storytellers. He has some delightful short stories and ten novels, the most well known being *Cloudstreet*, a story of two working-class families who suffer tragedy and are thrown together in the suburbs. It is a story of belonging, community and spirituality.[4] His writing richly evokes Australian characters and neighborhoods; it's a much more realistic and less parochial and caricatured picture of Australia than the popular movie *Crocodile Dundee*.

Tim's dad was a motorcycle cop. One day a drunk driver knocked him off his bike and through a wall. After weeks in a coma, he came home but was busted up and needed lots of help. Tim was horrified because his dad was like an augmented, earlier version of himself. It was difficult for his mother, because her husband was a big man. Tim recalls,

> Even though he was a little withered by the time in hospital, it was really difficult for her to bathe him. And I remember one day this bloke showed up at the front door. He just banged on the door and said, "Oh, g'day. My name's Len. I heard your hubby's a bit crook. Anything I can do?" He just showed up, and he used to, um, he used to carry my dad from bed and put him in the bath and he used to bathe him, which in the '60s in Perth in the suburbs was not the sort of thing you saw every day.
>
> It turned out that this bloke, Len Thomas, was from a local church and he'd heard that the old man was sick, and he thought he'd come and help out. And this weird, kind of strangely sacrificial act, where he'd come and wash another grown man and carry him to bed and look after him in a way that Mum just physically couldn't do. Something, you know, it really touched me, in that regardless of theology or anything else, watching a grown man bother, for nothing, to show up and wash a sick man . . . you know, it really affected me and, um . . . and gave me some stories.[5]

Len's neighborliness gave Tim inspiration for writing, but it also demonstrated to a young Tim how practical faith can inspire neighborly action. It is not just we Aussies who are impressed by this sort of quiet help for a neighbor or friend who is down and out. We all need the sense of belonging and the support of a community that comes alongside us and offers us a safe place.

Three decades later, Tim wrote a short story about neighbors helping a friend who needed a safe place.[6] Raelene, the central character, lives in a trailer park with two attention-starved daughters and an abusive husband. Sherry and Dan arrive in town and befriend her. Raelene tries to shock Sherry with stories of her sex life, but Sherry is unshockable and counters with acceptance, interest and her own stories of passionate intimacy with her husband. When Raelene talks of the violence in the home, Sherry is slow to give advice. Conversations with her new neighbor help Raelene feel good about herself.

Raelene comes to realize that Sherry and Dan are special because of their faith. She considers whether they are fakers, but doubts it. She watches them closely, intrigued and jealous. She is attracted by what she sees in their lives but wonders how it could be the same for her. She finds a Bible and reads it, but is frustrated with parts that she finds boring or impossible to understand.

Dan and Sherry accept Raelene's distaste of hypocrisy and her outright distrust of religion. As she rants, they nod more than argue. When Raelene asks if their lack of alcohol is because they are churchy, Dan admits he is a recovering alcoholic. Their capacity to honestly share their own struggles and need for God helps build a safe place for Raelene. She warms to the idea of Jesus and forgiveness, but struggles with other questions. They do not profess to have all the answers, but are open to a conversation. There is no artificial evangelism format, no help from a minister or other hired holy person, not even a reference to attending church. Rather Raelene's turning toward God and wholeness is inspired by the natural friendship from Sherry and Dan and by the safe place they offer to explore faith and consider a fresh start.

SAFE PLACES OF EVANGELISM

How can we foster safe places to nurture faith while avoiding inappropriate and unauthentic evangelism? How can we help people understand who Jesus is? As we are being incarnational—that is, being present in a community and practicing proximity with people—how do we proclaim that Christ is Lord?

This is a big challenge for any church, including churches that have made the shift from a consumer mentality to embracing their sentness. Missional churches sometimes have their imagination captured by a broader understanding of mission and get excited about service and justice, but are unsure about evangelism. Some people's understanding of holistic mission becomes not deed and word (as it should be), but deed and maybe word. We need safe places to offer people compassion and advocate for justice, but we also need places that are safe for people to explore who Jesus is and what that means for us.

We need non-McDonaldized ways of talking about the gospel (as well as expressing church) for different sorts of people.[7] Each person's sharing will be different, and the things we invite people to will be different, because people have different starting points and are at different points in the journey of faith. They may feel God is distant or they may be plagued by guilt; they may long for meaning or be working hard to overachieve or feel their lives are messed up beyond help. They may think they have it all together on their own, thanks very much.[8]

We do not have a ten-step evangelism plan. Maybe it would be nice if we did. Maybe not. But what we do have to share are a few powerful things that we believe help cultivate a spiritual search.

Curious questions. First, ask curious questions. Rather than speaking about what we believe or want to convince someone of, we start with questions to find out what they believe and what they have already experienced of God. We want to find out where people are coming from and ask questions that provoke their thinking. Let's plant seeds with questions rather than first giving information.

David Tacey, an associate professor at La Trobe University, researches the growing popularity of diverse spiritualities in Australia. Rather than dismissing this "spirituality revolution" as heretical or superficial, Tacey sees clues to how churches can respond to the cry for spiritual meaning. He challenges churches to be attentive and to listen to how God is communicating with people outside churches. We need to draw it out of people rather than trying to pump it in.[9]

We need to ask questions if we are to function as any kind of spiritual companion. Pastor and author Dan Kimball says he has never been knocked by people when he asks to have a coffee with them for an hour to ask about their impressions of Christianity and the church. Let's use questions to invite people into conversation about faith and to discover where people are at. We are not seeking arguments, but conversations about what really matters.

We collect good questions to use in different contexts. Here are some of our favorites:

- Where are you on your spiritual journey?
- Do you have a religious background?
- What were your earliest impressions of who God might be?
- What keeps you going when things are tough?
- Has there been a time in your life when you felt God was closest?
- What are some of your biggest issues with Christians today?
- What do you think about prayer and whether it does anything?
- Do you reckon there is any overall meaning and purpose to life?[10]

These ask about important issues. And we have learned not to underestimate people's interest in spiritual matters and their openness to talk about their perceptions and experiences of God. Many people are hungry for meaning and spirituality; they just do not necessarily look to the church for answers or for space to explore questions.

And when questions are asked back, we do not need to know all the answers ourselves. When we don't know something, let's admit it. When we don't have all the answers, people will be able to relate to that. Rick Richardson, an experienced campus worker and evangelism professor at Wheaton College, comments, "In the past, being an expert and having the answers were what built credibility and a hearing. Today, having the same questions, struggles and hurts is what builds credibility and gains a hearing."[11]

At Forge we like to allow grace and space for mystery, doubt and theological questioning. It is appropriate to stand for truth but also appropriate to allow space for others to question truth. Some say they left the church because it dismissed their questions or insisted on absolutes in areas that seemed nonessential to them. New Zealand pastor and sociologist Alan Jamieson studied why people leave evangelical, Pentecostal and charismatic churches. He relates their journeys to James Fowler's stages of faith development and says we need leaver-sensitive churches and liminal groups where leavers can explore their questions and emotions safely.[12] This is part of the value of seeing evangelism as a conversation that includes exploring questions and dilemmas, rather than simply communicating doctrinal information.

Stories. It is natural, after asking questions and hearing other people's opinions and experience, that you share something of your story. The most influential story you can share is your own. Let's never be embarrassed about this faith aspect of our life. Peter urged the early church, "You must worship Christ as Lord of your life. And if someone asks you about your Christian hope, always be ready to explain it. But do this in a gentle and respectful way" (1 Peter 3:15-16).

Remember the impact your way of life can have. In the recent past, the integrity of the *message* was primary. We were eager evangelists, memorizing answers to objections about faith to ensure we had the message straight and had logical responses to questions all sorted out. That is not unimportant. But nowadays the integrity of the messenger is primary. People look at the pattern of our lives before the proclamation of our words, so they will more likely grasp truth as we live submerged among them, authentically sharing our stories.

This doesn't mean we all need spectacular testimonies. Where have we experienced God for ourselves? Where are we growing in our faith? Where have we struggled and come through with the help of Jesus? Sri Lankan evangelist Ajith Fernando warns, "Christians who do not know the joys of lingering in the presence of God will be at a loss to know how to respond when people speak of serenity through New Age disciplines like transcendental meditation."[13]

What is an experience of God that you can authentically share? What is it that captured your imagination about what really is good news about Jesus? What has Jesus done for and in you? Your story and experience of God is worth sharing. And your friends, even when they have a different background, will likely be interested in your faith as part of who you are. Don't undersell it. In sharing your story and experience of God, rather than just ideas or beliefs about God, you are more likely to encourage people in their own spiritual search. Let your story invite people toward experiences of God, not just ideas about God.

Don't underestimate how interested people are in experiencing God. A Christian student was witnessing on a secular university campus to a New Age friend. The Christian girl had gone through her arsenal of Christian apologetics without sensing any break-through. They were about to part when the Christian said, "Before you go, can I pray for you?" She began to pray and was surprised to find the New Age girl crying. "I just can't believe you're speaking to God!" she said.[14] Your experience of God will speak volumes.

Centered-set communities. Consumer culture thinks in mass terms—we are not diverse people congregated together but categories of people organized in homogenous units. Historically this has led to in-groups and out-groups, with those who don't fit the dominant category marginalized and neglected. A culture organized around incarnational mission looks at the world differently: the place of comfort is a place to search for new friends, to pursue those who have been dismissed as beyond the reach of a loving God.

Groups invite people to belong based on different criteria, called bounded sets or centered sets.[15] Bounded-set groups use clear boundaries. People are "in" or "out" depending on their beliefs and behavior, on being on a membership roll or on whether they hold a commitment to a specific ideology. In contrast, centered sets don't define people as in or out but measure their proximity to a defined center: a Christian, for example, under a centered-set perspective is someone who has made Jesus the center of his or her life and is growing in Jesus' direction. Frost and Hirsch illustrate the difference by talking about wells and fences. Some farmers build fences around their properties to keep their livestock in and others' livestock out (a bounded set). But remote farmers do not waste time with fences. They dig a well, knowing cattle will stay close to the water supply (a centered set).

Centered-set evangelism seeks to tantalize not-yet Christians into a process of searching and encourages everyone to grow in faith and Christlikeness. It assumes the Spirit is drawing all people to God and that we all long to know the reason for our existence. All are welcomed into relationship with a missionary people, and all who have experienced the shift are encouraged to support and encourage one another as they seek shalom with those outside the gates of acceptability. This space making often results not in a homogenous community but a fellowship of freaks—an eclectic group captivated by and centered on Jesus.

Churches as centered-set safe places are not concerned with artificial boundaries and adopting cultural habits, but recognize that Christ the living water is so precious that people will want to center their lives on him. We love interactive and participatory worship, and when we lead and preach we tend not to dominate the microphone. We like to invite anyone and everyone to participate in worship to whatever extent they like. Some people may simply sit and listen; others are keen to share about their journey and experience. We try to cultivate church life as a context that is safe for people to share from their heart, including people with different perspectives and people who are still on a journey toward faith.

This is contentious in some circles, including some churches that are only starting to embrace their sentness. They sometimes get nervous when people outside traditional boundaries are permitted to contribute in church. We have heard of parent churches that try to stop new experimental church plants from letting people who are not Christians lead singing or participate in other ways. An open mic is dangerous to the status quo, our friends have found.

We are less concerned with whether people believe the "right" things or behave in the "right" way *before* they participate and more concerned that we are welcoming them in the right way and helping guide them to explore in Jesus' direction. We are inspired to make the well available, and if people want to taste and take a drink and to talk about how they are finding the journey, we give them a microphone. We expect to learn something along the way as well as help others in their journey.[16]

People are after a loving, genuine community, not just ideas about God. People long for love and for a safe place to belong. That is an apologetic that will win Hindus in India, Muslims in Iran, agnostics in Europe, secularists in Australia and lapsed believers in America. Our world needs churches prepared to offer safe places to people in need of refuge.

JOINING GOD AT AA

The need for safe places extends beyond corporate worship. There are children in our neighborhoods who need safe places in other people's homes. Our churches need to advocate for these children. Children cannot thrive when they live in fear, and the church should be leading the charge for foster care and adoption. Our close friends and Forge staff members, Brad and Michelle and Clark and Carrisa, are two couples who went through foster-parent training and opened their homes to children in need. Both sets of parents will tell you how it has changed their lives and the lives of the children they foster.

Which other groups in our neighborhoods and our world need our voices to speak up for them? Shawn was doing a residency with Forge Dallas and had a desire to start a Christian support group for addicts and alcoholics. He had attended a number of Alcoholics Anonymous meetings and recovery groups over the years. He thought maybe God wanted him to create a safe Christian place for people struggling with addictions.

Addiction is the biggest public health issue in the West. In the United States, 22.1 million people (8.7 percent of the population) have a substance abuse or dependency problem. Of these, 17.9 million (7 percent) are alcohol abusers or alcoholics.[17] Two million Americans have a gambling addiction and another four to six million are problem gamblers.[18] Fifteen million Americans are addicted to pornography, including an increasing number of teenagers and pastors.[19] All addictions have negative effects on relationships and families. But how prepared are we to deal with compulsive behaviors? Causes and treatment for addiction are complex. How safe and supportive are our faith communities?

As Shawn journeyed through the residency, he started asking a key question: "God, where are you at work, and in light of my gifts and resources, how can I join you?" The paradigm change for Shawn came when he realized God had been at work in the nonreligious AA meetings he used to attend. So he made the decision to make himself available to God and to people involved in the meetings.

Through participating regularly in his local AA meetings, Shawn has been able to grow many friendships and is coming alongside people in AA who are hurting and struggling. He is continuing to ask what is actually good news for people struggling with addiction and how he can cooperate with God in showing his love to people he meets. He says,

> The beautiful thing about AA is that it is a group of people that are brought together by their brokenness to help one another. Being connected with AA groups has given me the opportunity to connect with people, learn from others, and has given me the opportunity to bless and help those who are hurting who might never walk through the doors of a church building.[20]

Sean Gladding, who copastored Mercy Street in Houston, said they learned a lot from AA and the twelve-step process about being a safe place for people struggling with addictions.[21] Alcoholics Anonymous has high expectations of people—they disciple or "sponsor" people who want to change, and they call on people to commit themselves to name and seek release and recovery from their bondage. Along the way, however, they are a supportive community without shame. They provide a safe place for people to share their experiences and solve problems in a nonjudgmental environment. A member of AA in the 1940s, Jerome Ellison, wrote about the need to be honest with one another about our weaknesses:

> The relief of being accepted can never be known by one who never thought himself unaccepted. I hear of "good Christian men and women" belonging to "fine old church families."

There were no good Christians in the first church, only sinners. Peter never let himself or his hearers forget his betrayal in the hour the cock crowed. James, stung by the memory of his years of stubborn resistance, warned the church members: "Confess your faults to one another." That was before there were fine old church families. Today the last place where one can be candid about one's faults is in church. In a bar, yes, in a church, no. I know; I've tried both places. Let that sting you and me just as it should, and make us miserable with our church Pharisaism till we see it is just as definite and just as hideous as anybody's drunkenness can ever be, and a great deal more really dangerous.[22]

A supportive community without shame that calls on people to commit themselves to name and seek release and recovery from their bondage—this is church at its best.

BEING SAFE FOR CURIOUS VISITORS

At the end of my (Darren) first year at Auburn, Claire and Shane announced, "We would like to be baptized this Sunday." I was surprised; this was a big step for this immigrant couple. I warmly congratulated them, but also applauded Auburn for offering a safe place of welcoming and hospitality to these curious visitors.

In the beginning, Shane had fears from his religious background that our church members might be violent to them. So when they first came to Auburn, Shane sent Claire in first and was ready with his cell phone to call the police. To their surprise, however, the church welcomed them: people talked to them, the pastor smiled, and Claire washed dishes with ninety-year-old Eunice. *Part of being church as a safe place for Auburn is taking turns helping in the kitchen.*

On the next Sunday, Rob and Mat talked with them about Christianity's distinctives and encouraged them to read about Jesus in the

Gospels. And Tim and Beth invited them to our neighboring Nite Church at Kew. *Part of being church as a safe place for Auburn is cooperating with neighboring churches.*

On the third Sunday, Claire and Shane joined Jenni, Lainey and Johannes to lay hands on Eunice and pray for her health. They had asked about a Bible the week before, so Tim and Mary both gave them Bibles. Someone else had also tracked down a Bible in their native language. *Part of being church as a safe place for Auburn is seeing what needs doing and doing it without a fuss.*

They shared lunch with a few new friends from church, and that Sunday we went to Nite Church and heard an announcement about Bible studies. So on the fourth Sunday, Claire and Shane asked whether Auburn has Bible studies. By then they had read most of the Gospels. After gatherings, they were among the last to leave, because they were eager to discuss Christianity with David and others. *Part of being church as a safe place for Auburn is discussing faith, both in and after worship gatherings.*

The next month, Auburn prayed for Lainey and Johannes as they went to Indonesia. Shane and Claire saw that Jesus does not call people just for their own benefit but to serve others. Claire and Shane are catching the calling Jesus prayed for us: "Just as you sent me into the world, I am sending them into the world" (John 17:18). They have a desire to serve the world and make a difference in the lives of people on the margins. They are getting a vision of being *sent* as Jesus-followers into the world—here in our Melbourne suburb or perhaps other parts of the world, such as their home country. *Part of being church as a safe place for Auburn is sending one another with our blessing to serve the world around us.*

Later that month, Yvonne and the Yarra Gospel Choir taught Shane and Claire what became their favorite song, "Shine." They finished reading the New Testament, they helped collect Christmas gifts through Camcare, and Sue and Rob invited them home for

Christmas lunch. *Part of being church as a safe place for Auburn is including one another.*

After Christmas, Shane and Claire asked what is involved in becoming a follower of Jesus. I met once a week (often twice) to discuss Christianity and baptism with Claire and Shane, as well as David, Joanna, Jessie, Mary, Lainey, Rob and Johannes. As everyone shared their experience of God, Claire and Shane discovered experientially that God has come close in Jesus Christ and that baptism is not the end of the journey but the beginning. They amazed the group with their descriptions of what it was like to start to seek God in their country of origin and with their fresh insights and growing faith. *Part of being church as a safe place for Auburn is learning from one another.*

The church realized afresh that baptism is not just Jesus connecting with individuals, but Jesus calling someone to identify with him and his body—the church. Claire and Shane said the person of Jesus attracted them—especially the person of Jesus they saw in new friends at Auburn. Claire said, "The first time I came to church I imagined Jesus with open arms. And step by step I could see Jesus in all of you." *Part of being church as a safe place for Auburn is people seeing Jesus in our lives.*

Early the next year, Claire and Shane were baptized. Since then they have continued to discover the adventure of faith and church. They have moved to another city, and we pray they continue to know the benefit of church as a safe place and as a breeding ground for dangerous stories. We cheer on Claire and Shane for finding life in Jesus, and we cheer on Auburn for living the good news. It takes a community being church and offering a safe place to lead a person to Christ.[23]

Rusty the Contractor

Greg Hunt, lead pastor at Paseo Christian Church and director of Border Forge in El Paso, has been coaching Rusty, a Border Forge resident.[24] Rusty might not be an ideal theological school student, but he is an ideal Forge resident. He is not much of a reader of the latest missional books—in fact, he is not much of a reader of anything. He does not hog the conversation in groups; he does not share much at all. But Rusty is a great missionary.

One day Rusty said to Greg, "I'm sorry. I probably won't be at Sunday morning gatherings much anymore. Will you pray for me though?" He is planning on hosting a brunch with his workers, his family and others. His missional goal—or the way he expresses what he wants to do—is "to provide Sabbath and to listen and to be ready to pray like the pub guy in that shaping book."[25]

At his business, Rusty intentionally hires "derelicts"—not a very nice word, we know, but a word people sometimes use to refer to people with huge and multiple problems. By hiring ex-convicts, many of whom are struggling with addictions, Rusty adds value to their resumes because "everyone needs a tenth chance."

Recently Rusty hired Larry. Larry is not a loner—he has a wife and five children, ages three to twelve. He is also a heroin/crack addict and worked as a drug runner. He has done time in jail for a number of offences related to his involvement with drugs. Because of Larry's ways, his family was not well supported. They had no money, no food and no means of transport. You get the picture. For accommodations, they were living in a domestic violence shelter. Rusty organized for friends from Paseo to provide for some basic needs of the five children. He wants not just to be Larry's boss but a "blessing" to him and the other workers at Rusty's business.

Rusty's "project" with Border Forge is to invest in this family and other families of the men who work for his contracting business—to figure out and implement community development with his workers and to rally the church community around them. His first agenda is not to invite them *to* church. Instead he engages himself within his everyday work context and seeks to *be* the church.

We need church to be a safe place, not just within the walls of our buildings and gatherings, but wherever the people of God are seeking to be the church. While others walk away, our role is to walk toward. That is what Jesus does. We love that about him. And we are challenged to be sent and to send others to foster the same kinds of safe places in the dangerous stories Jesus is telling through the church.

6

SHARED LIFE

And all the believers met together in one place
and shared everything they had.

ACTS 2:44

When we have no impressive buildings and no swollen budgets
to sustain our work, often only then do we realize that the best
we have to offer this post-Christendom world is the quality
of our relationships, the power of our trustworthiness,
and the wonder of our generosity.

MICHAEL FROST

THERE I SAT, IN A CHAIR IN THE TATTOO PARLOR, gazing at the assorted pictures and photos across the walls. Each one represented a mark on some person's body. Some were intricate and meaningful, others angry and violent, still others just silly. I (Kim) handed the artist a piece of paper with my choice for my tattoo: one word, *diatribo*.

"What's it say?" he asked, then tried to pronounce it.

"It's Greek," I said.

"What's it mean?" he asked.

"It literally means 'to rub between, to rub hard.' For me it means a shared life."

The artist smiled and began to prepare the apparatus. I am sure he had heard thousands of explanations for why people put particular words on their skin. "Which way do you want it?" he asked. "Facing out, or is it for you to read?"

"This one's for me."

"Why this word?" he asked casually.

Why this word? It was used in the Bible to reflect shared life abiding with one another, skin rubbing up against skin. Jesus shared his life with a small group of people. This incredible, kind, wise, loving teacher stuck with a bunch of young scalawags. And, along the way, who he was—his character, his nature—rubbed off on them.

I want to be like Jesus. I want to give my life to helping others. I want people to experience his grace and love and peace. I want Jesus to rub off of me and on to others, and I want Jesus to rub off of others and on to me.

Diatribo is one of my favorite words in the Bible. The English translations—"stayed with," "abided with"—are insufficient to describe this sacred transaction between people. *Diatribo* is a way of life led by the Savior. I want to live with the same sacrificial purpose—that any good that God has redeemed in me and through me would graciously and generously rub off on others. It reminds me to give priority to relationships and to stay with the people God puts me with, even and maybe especially when staying is hard, when staying hurts.

I love people deeply. All people. A counselor once told me that I feel not only my pain but also the pain of everyone in the room. I believe and see the best in people, and I make a habit of telling them how valuable they are.

I am not the smartest person in the Forge Mission Training Network. In fact, I am in awe of the authors and international consultants and world-famous preachers I get to work with. However, I have always known I was put on the earth to love others, not with some nominal, superficial, religious love but with love like Christ's love, a giving of life for others.

I was taught that way of loving as a young Christian. I have connected easily with Forge's idea of shared life and discipleship, and mission as a way of life not a program, because that is how I experienced it firsthand as a young person; the youth leader couple in my church invested in me and shared their lives. They were like the big brother and sister I never had. I will always cherish their mentoring of me.

My youth pastor, Steve Swain, took me under his wing and spent time both teaching me about life and showing me how to live. He and his wife, Sonia, opened their home, fed me and let me sleep over when I needed to. Even their kids embraced me; I was best man in their oldest son's wedding.

Steve was no pushover; there were many tears and hard conversations between us. I could not lie to him, because he knew all my thoughts. I'd sit in his office, sweating excessively, as he asked me questions I had no answers to. Steve is one of the most stubborn, straight-talking, confrontational people I have ever met.

Beyond opening his home to me and teaching me about Jesus, Steve took me all over Australia and even overseas to experience the mission of the church firsthand. He taught me to talk to kids in the local high school about Jesus and to love those who were slowly finding their way back to God. He gave me my first opportunity to preach in a church—when I was sixteen.

I wanted to do what Steve did, so when I was eighteen, I became a pastor and got to work with him as his assistant youth pastor. When I was twenty, Steve walked my wife down the aisle at our wedding (Maria's father had passed away several years before). When I was twenty-four, we dreamed together and took the plunge into church planting as we started The Junction. We all knew it would be different, because Steve is different, but we never knew how different it would be from your standard church plant.

The mentoring and discipleship that Steve gave me shaped my view of Jesus and how I should follow him. For the first part of our marriage, Maria and I poured ourselves into the lives of the young people at our local church and then into the young adults and families of our new church plant. We opened our home and ate regularly with people. Whether it was refugees or newlyweds, we gave people time. We shared life with them. And this is how we live our life today.

When I came to the United States to lead Forge America and work with grassroots missionaries, megachurches and multisite churches, I wanted to have the same posture. I don't want to belong to a friendly church that doesn't see life as something to be shared. I want the people of God to find and build friendships—lifelong ones. I value shared life.

This is one of the most intangible yet valuable postures of a missionary. It's discipleship in its simplest form. As Mike Breen, director of 3DM, says, the missional church will die without discipleship. Mike and his wife, Sally, lead their organization as if it were their family. That is the ethos of shared life we need in our churches and in our missional teams.

In November 2012 Brad Brisco, a church-planting strategist in Kansas and a Forge team member, developed what he thought was influenza: headaches, chills and a fever. It got scarier for Brad and his wife, Michelle, when he became incoherent. So she rushed him to a hospital, where Brad, with his brain swelling, was treated for suspected bacterial meningitis. Then the doctor thought it was viral encephalitis meningitis. Really, they were not exactly sure what it was.

This otherwise fit and healthy man couldn't speak or remember his last name. In treatment things looked grim. They thought he faced long-term rehabilitation and potentially lasting disabilities. After a grueling two weeks, he started taking two steps forward, one step back.

It is times like those you need shared life with a tribe who can look out for you. Ryan and Laura Hairston, our Forge Dallas directors, organized meals for Michelle and the boys. We had international prayer meetings online. I flew to Kanas City and went straight to the hospital. Brad had just been through a spinal tap, which is painful, and I held his hand. He cried as he said, "Kimmy, I am so sorry for what Carter has gone through."

"It's all right, Brad," I said.

I asked how Lance (Brad's best friend and coworker in Forge Kansas City) was doing. Brad described to me the first time Lance came to visit at his bedside in the hospital. Brad could not say much, because he was still recovering. Lance is a true Texan, with a heart of gold, but did not say much either, because there was not much you can say at times like that. Lance simply took Brad's head, held it to his chest and said, "I'm scared. I don't want you to die." And the two men cried because they share life and love each other. Lance, his son Jordan and another pastor took out oil, anointed Brad and prayed for their sick friend.

It turned out to be West Nile disease, so it was treatable. The good news is that Brad has recovered well, with no lasting ramifications. Two months later, Brad and Michelle adopted a baby girl.

We all long for community. We all need friends who will take our head to their chest and tell us they love us when we are at our lowest.

JESUS SHARING LIFE

Jesus modeled this notion of shared life for us wonderfully in his friendship with his disciples and in his acceptance of support from them. We don't have to spend much time reading the Gospels to see that Jesus is sold out on sharing life with his community. Look just at the Gospel of John. It starts with Jesus' commitment to sharing life with us on earth. John 1:14 tells us that, amazingly, Jesus, the Word, became human and lived here on earth among us.

Before long, Jesus' ministry was rubbing off on John the Baptist's disciples, who were worried that Jesus was baptizing and attracting people away from them (John 3:25-26). What would that do to their ministry? But John had a bigger perspective than his disciples. He confronted their consumer orientation, which had them seeing Jesus as competition.

John described his relationship to Jesus in terms of intimate friendship. He explained that he had come not as the Messiah but as the one sent ahead of the Messiah—as best man to the groom (vv. 28-29). John understood his sentness. He was not the central figure but there to serve. He was celebrating the success and future of the bridegroom and all that the future held for him and his bride.

John also celebrated the goodness and generosity of God, who provides "plenty of water" (v. 23) and who gives God's "Spirit without limit" (v. 34). He says, "The Father loves his Son and has put everything into his hands" (v. 35). And the Son, Jesus, shares all the life he has with his disciples.

Jesus loves us and wants to give us eternal life forever. But part of the good news that is often overlooked is that Jesus wants to share life with us now—and invites us to share life with his community.

Jesus understood the importance of sharing life. He did not just care for those who were close to him; he also loved sharing life with them. We know Jesus loves the whole world. Jesus loves the nations. Jesus loved his nation of Israel. Jesus loved the crowds who drew close to listen to his teaching, and he loved those who ignored him. Jesus loved the circle of seventy-two disciples, but he especially loved the twelve disciples. And he especially loved and leaned on the three who were often closest at hand—Peter, James and John.

John is described as the disciple Jesus loved and as the one who had leaned back against Jesus at the Last Supper, leaning on his chest—or on his breast, as the King James Version translates it. John asked, "Lord, who will betray you?" (John 21:20). When Jesus was at his lowest, when he was anticipating his greatest challenge and facing his deepest disappointments, he drew strength from a friend who drew close and spoke to his heart. So, for Jesus, discipleship included shared life.

This rubbing of life on life is the core of what it means to be a disciple of a missionary God. Jesus entered into the lives of strangers and formed a band of brothers and sisters. If the church simply did this in our day, we would radically change the world.

Jesus showed his commitment to *diatribo* in his prayers for us. There it is in red, John 17:20-23, where we get an inside picture of what Jesus says and prays about us. It can be a beautiful thing to overhear when someone says nice things about you when they think you are not there. Here Jesus advocates for you and for your community with our Father in heaven:

> I am praying not only for these disciples but also for all who will ever believe in me through their message. I pray that they will all be one, just as you and I are one—as you are in me, Father, and I am in you. And may they be in us so that the world will believe you sent me. I have given them the glory you gave me, so they may be one as we are one. I am in them and you are in me. May they experience such perfect unity that the world will know that you sent me and that you love them as much as you love me. (John 17:20-23)

A God who shares life as Father, Son and Spirit grabs our imagination. God offers to share that life with us and invites us to share it with one another. How we express our shared life is part of how people see the reality of who God is. Part of our witness is through the quality of our relationships and our unity. Jesus prayed we would reflect the interconnectedness and mutuality of God in the loving dance of Father, Son and Spirit.

REMEMBER THE TITANS

Remember the Titans is a football movie set in 1971 in Virginia in a recently desegregated high school. As a product of their time, the Titans are a team in name only; they are plagued by racial tension and discrimination. The appointment of African American head coach Herman Boone (played by Denzel Washington) seems a brave move by the school, but he is resisted by some of the players and, for most of the movie, by the school board. Nevertheless, he leads the team in rigorous training and coaxes then to get to know and understand one another.

During football camp, he wakes the whole team at three in the morning and goads them to the site of the Battle of Gettysburg. There he gives a rousing speech about the effects of hatred. That is where the school board starts to try to get rid of him. But the Titans go through the season undefeated, overcoming their prejudice and helping the broader community see beyond segregation. As they share life across ethnic divides, they meld as a team.

We are glad God has called us to follow Jesus, but we are also very glad he does not call us to follow alone. Praise God for community! We need one another. We regularly tell our churches that we are glad we do not serve God alone but in community with them. As the church, we belong to one another, in all our multicultural, multiage, multi-faith-stage diversity. We appreciate and value the diversity of ages, genders, backgrounds, faith stages and cultures that are represented in the church.

Diatribo, or shared life, is not a new idea. Fellowship has been a part of the church's DNA from the beginning. Movements throughout church history have brought the people of God into deeper relationships around missional life. Wesley started accountability groups; Neil Cole rebranded them Life Transformation Groups. Gilbert Bilezikian wrote *Community 101*, in which he explains that community is not an invention of the church but an expression of God's trinitarian self.[1] When we share life in deep community, we are exposed to Jesus, who dwells in each of us. We don't just facilitate a program of the modern church; we literally reflect the Godhead in its trinitarian relationship.

One of the greatest acts of evangelism is the demonstration of love and forgiveness. A handshake between two strangers during a greeting time in a service is not in itself powerful. But the messy, real, shared life of love and forgiveness between people is. When the world sees genuine tolerance, grace, love and acceptance, they witness something supernatural and otherworldly. When people experience true community through the body of Christ, it's not that there is never conflict but that there is real resolution, love and forgiveness.

In our society, people often fail to feel the pain of others. We get busy with life. We treasure our emotional boundaries. And in contradiction to Jesus' invitation to sentness, we protect our churches from the rub, especially with people outside the walls of the church. Busyness with insider activities further erodes the church's witness in the world as well as the experience of "life to the full" that Jesus came to bring us.

When sentness has been embraced, however, groups of people who may not have much else in common come together around the missional DNA and shared life. They form a bond beyond social status and racial identity. There is no magic bullet, special new program or one way to do missional church; a sent community is held together by its commitment to the strength of its relationships.

Kim has worked for Forge since 2003, and Darren has been involved since 2005. Neither of us has ever been full time with Forge.

In fact, Forge has never employed anyone full time. Forge has never owned anything of value. We have never had permanent offices or national headquarters. If you ask people involved in Forge where it is, they'll tell you it's in their house or basement or cubicle on loan from a denomination or megachurch. But what they're really telling you is that the work of Forge—the work of any missionary movement—is located in the relationships it participates in.

Simply put, people who have embraced their identities as people of God on mission with God give their life to the mission of God and to the people they meet along the way. They have found a tribe that shares life. *Diatribo.*

This is not to say that we have achieved some exalted level of relationship that eludes less missional churches. We don't do some things well at all. Nevertheless, we love our tribe—the people who have gathered together around the mission God has given us. We love them with our lives, and if we can serve them in some way, we do.

In different contexts, we have met leaders who build complex teams with multiple levels of volunteers that lack *diatribo*. They recruit people who are giving their lives to the organization. We are struck, however, when these people do not love one another. The leaders see the volunteers (and even some of the staff) as worker bees, building their hive. The volunteers (and even some of the staff) see the leaders as figureheads or dictators. They don't see one another as whole persons. They don't share life in any way other than in a series of meetings and services. Their relationship would not be described as *diatribo*. They are not friends or even colaborers; they are ships that pass in the night.

When we set out on a mission with people, we want *diatribo* with and between us. We get to know each other's spouses and kids. We eat in one another's homes. We are as generous as we can be. We want to do the same with those we serve and love and lead. We want everyone we mentor and disciple, everyone we partner with in God's mission, to experience this kind of community, because it is a way to experience the character and nature of God. We want to live this way because Jesus did.

CARRIED OR CARRYING?

Mark 2 is a great story of healing and salvation for a crippled man to whom Jesus gives forgiveness and the ability to walk again. But we invite you to read it a little differently—as a great story of sharing life and friendship.

When Jesus returned to Capernaum, "the news spread quickly that he was back home" (v. 1). Jesus was respected as a teacher and rabbi, but he taught like no other rabbi. He was so good at his stuff that when he stood up in synagogues and in the temple, people were astounded at the authority with which he taught. And yet he went from teaching in those holy places to going and eating meals with people who were considered sinful, corrupt and questionable characters.

The Jews of Jesus' day could not put Jesus in a box. He was profound, not just in his teaching but also in his behavior and relationships—in the ways he related to women, to children, to the marginalized. When he came to town, people came out as a crowd to see and hear him.

As a result, "soon the house where he was staying was so packed with visitors that there was no more room, not even outside the door" (v. 2). This seemed to be a "successful" event. People were gathering and hearing good news. But it was not connecting for everyone. Sometimes crowds and gatherings can help us connect with Jesus. But just as often crowds can stop or at least limit us from experiencing community. Sometimes we hide in crowds. Sometimes the crowd keeps us from getting to Jesus. Sometimes there is someone in the crowd we are offended or upset with, and we focus on that person rather than Jesus.

But the crowd did not keep four people carrying their friend—a paralyzed man—from getting to Jesus. The Bible does not actually tell us they are friends. But it doesn't seem likely that they were four strangers who saw a crippled man and said to one another, "Hey, let's carry this dude to Jesus." Like good friends, they met him where he was at and sought to help him get where he needed to be.

Contrast these friends with the friends of Job. When he was at his lowest and might have felt most abandoned by God, they thought it was an ideal time to share their "wisdom." When Job most needed friends to cry with him and hold him to their chest, they started dishing out advice about what he had done wrong and what he needed to do to get right with God. When we are most debilitated, we can do without being judged. But we can't do without friends who say, "What can I do to carry a little bit of the load?"

This guy was fortunate to have four such friends. Each picked up a corner of his mat, and they carried him to Jesus. If you underline one sentence in this chapter, underline this: *Meet people where they are at.* Don't judge them. Don't solve problems for them. You are not Jesus. Simply carry them to Jesus. Jesus is the only one who can solve their problems—you can't. Community is at its best when we play our part to help carry struggling friends. When we act with that kind of friendship, there is space for something supernatural to happen.

Who do you identify with in this story? You might identify with the people who are carrying their friend. Do you tend to carry others, or do you know someone who does? Are you a person who everyone talks to, who asks others how they are doing but rarely gets asked? Are you a person who helps, cooks, babysits, assists? Are you a person people come to when they need to borrow something or want to ask something? Carriers simply serve, love, give and help by carrying other people's burdens.

Our wives are like this. Maria serves and cooks and loves without fame or fortune, never wanting to get on stage. She has opened our home to the kids on our street like they were her own. Whether it's feeding them, helping them with their homework or just loving them, she is an amazing example of love.

Jenni is a carrier too. She is great at asking curious questions and listening to people unburden themselves. In fact, she doesn't even have to ask questions; people just seem to discern that she is a good listener. When Jenni goes to the doctor, she even ends up listening to the doctor's problems.

But sometimes people who carry others become paralyzed. Sometimes they simply can't move. The causes of paralysis do not discriminate; sickness or sin, doubt or disaster can befall rich or poor, black or white, Latino or Asian. It is a fallacy of modern times to think that we can be self-sufficient all the time. There are times we can carry others, but also times when we need to be carried.

How can we embrace our sentness when we need to be carried? Can we live missionally only when we are carrying others? It's possible, in fact, when we always strive to be the carrier in a re-lationship, to reinforce a consumer Christianity that subverts the gospel. Christianity is about receiving grace as well as sharing it. Church is a gift to us as our community and tribe for shared mission and as a place for us to be there for others. Sometimes our ministry will be carrying others, but sometimes we will need others to carry us. That does not detract from our value or calling. Our dignity is not less if we need to be carried for a time or even throughout life.

Jean Vanier, who founded L'Arche, an international federation of homes and programs for people with intellectual disabilities, challenges our perspectives on this. The developmentally disabled and other chronically disabled people (or the members of our com-munity who are not functioning as missionaries) do not cease to have meaning, do not become only dead weight, just by virtue of needing the support of others. Nor do they cease to have responsibility to others.

You may have never gotten to a point of paralysis. But be prepared, because someday you may experience it. And when you do, you will be blessed to have friends around who have shared life with you and can pick up a corner of your mat and help carry you.

How do we know? That is what happened to me (Kim) and our family when Carter was diagnosed with cancer. Maria and I had never faced anything like it before. And we were paralyzed—not knowing what to do or how to move forward. We also were without our normal support structures.

After getting the news and starting to see how cancer affected my boy and what treatment he needed, I cried every day. I had come to America and was the national director of Forge and the director of missional imagination at one of the largest multisite churches in the country, but none of that mattered. I became a father paralyzed by grief.

For a thousand days I watched my son beaten; his hair fell out, his gums bled. I had to carry him, because he was so weak. Normally carrying others is part of our upbringing and family DNA. And it's our calling. But for the last few years, we needed to be carried. Maria and I lay down as paralyzed parents and were carried by the prayers and generosity of others.

Like the paralyzed man carried by his four friends, I am glad our friends didn't stop short of seeing us through. When the four friends got to the house where Jesus was teaching, it was full, and they couldn't get through to Jesus. But they didn't say, "Well, we have done our bit. We carried him for as long as we could, and that's enough. We'll leave now." They took friendship to another level, literally. They carried him onto the roof of someone else's house and dug through it. They didn't care about their clothes getting dirty.

When they looked through their newly built, custom-designed skylight, they looked through with grubby faces.

Friendship can get dirty. When we carry people, we get soiled. When you love someone, you get down on your hands and knees and get muddy for them. Isn't that what friends do?

These four friends kept telling themselves, "All we need to do is get him to Jesus." Having made the hole, they lowered the man down. "I trust you," he might have said. "Just don't drop me, OK?"

And Jesus responded to the faith of the man's friends, forgave his sins and healed his body.

When I travel now, others who have faced cancer often tell me about their experience. One woman got breast cancer in her fifties. She unburdened with her small group with whom she shared life. She told them honestly that she was not terrified about chemo and the treatments, but she was worried about losing her hair. She said that since she knew it was going to go, she would shave it off that night so it would go on her terms.

So she shaved it, bought a wig and went to her treatment. As she entered the hospital, her small group went in with her—and they had all shaved off their hair. They told her, "If people are going to stare, let them stare at all of us."

WE NEED YOU

Diatribo is not just what our churches or people we minister to need. We need it ourselves.

At the core of who we are, in terms of relationships and friendships, we all need others. When Jesus left earth, he invited us to be Christ to one another. Truly, we are completed by one another.

And we are a gift to one another. You may not think of people you do church or mission with as a gift. That might be because you don't know them enough or because you know them too much. No family is perfect, so maybe you have had a bad experience with a small group or church. But we are imperfect people called to share life. God uses our brokenness to bring us together to be Jesus to one another.

We need to take seriously how we share life with others. The dozens of "one another" imperatives in the Bible are not just because other people need us, but because we also need them. We need to consider our need for others as being just as valid as our support, care and nurture of them.

FRIENDS FOR US MISSIONARIES?

As we've looked around our churches and missional networks, we've grown to realize that it is the relationships that ride on and contribute to the success of our mission. In Forge we hang in with those who incarnate and contextualize the gospel in innovative ways, but if relationships are not right, we have to ask ourselves what we are communicating.

A blind spot is the thing we have that everyone else knows about and laughs about, but we do not know (or pretend not to know) why they are laughing. "What are you talking about?" we say. Can you think of something about someone else that you laugh about?

We all have things that annoy others and rub others the wrong way. You might be someone who avoids confrontation (like Kim), or you might love a good fight and its creative energies (like Darren). You might be passionate about one thing, but you are working with people whose passions lie in other areas. Maybe you value excellence and preparation, while your friend loves casual spontaneity. In case you haven't already realized it, not everyone else is like you. You will sometimes butt up against others. We are different and we see the world through our own lens. This is a big issue facing any team.

We like the way Australian poet Michael Leunig expresses thanks for friendships with realism about the struggles:

We give thanks for our friends
Our dear friends.
We anger each other.
We fail each other.
We share this sad earth, this tender life,
this precious time.
Such richness. Such wildness.
Together we are blown about.
Together we are dragged along.
All this delight.
All this suffering.
All this forgiving life.
We hold it together. Amen.[2]

We have high hopes for missional churches and the networks we work with. We want to see fresh mission-shaped dreaming and action to reach the Western world. We want to see churches planted and movements flourishing in America, Australia, Canada and throughout Europe. That is unlikely to happen if we, who are the basis of whatever the future of our churches and networks holds, don't realize and acknowledge our need for one another. And, frankly, if we don't get our heads around our relationships and how to love one another and be authentic friends, our teams and churches are not going to be attractive, healthy places—for us, let alone for others.

It becomes critically important when things are difficult that we lean on people with whom we have been sharing life. We expect kids to have close friendships and to value them. One cartoon shows a child reading off a list: "Fourteen people love me, twenty-two people like me, six people tolerate me, and I have only three enemies. Not bad for a little kid, huh?" But as grownups we are expected to put that kind of calculation behind us and get on with items of supposed greater consequence. When we face disappointments or are plagued by loneliness or depression or are questioning our faith, however, we need friends we can turn to.

A large portion of my (Darren's) discretionary time as a child was taken up with shared activities with friends. I loved hanging out with my friends in primary school. We rode Billy carts and bikes, played hide-and-seek and talked about girls and our favorite band, Rose Tattoo. In high school my mode of transport changed to horses, we discussed more religion and politics, and we listened to Midnight Oil. During my university days, I got more serious about God and ministry, later got married and had children, moved too much, sought to accomplish too much and collected too many degrees. I see in hindsight that I have had less room for friendship than I had in school. Perhaps that is appropriate for the stage of life I'm in. But maybe it is also an adult and especially masculine view that sees friends as a nice add-on but not necessary to the real stuff of life.[3]

Steve Biddulph's book *Manhood* has helped remind us of the importance of making space for friendship. There is plenty that works against this among men in society—individualism, fear of homosexuality (or the appearance of it), toughness, masks, the example of remote fathers and especially competitiveness. Biddulph says,

> Competition is the bane of men's lives. To this day, when I sit down in a public place, beside a swimming pool, for example, I relax and feel good if there is no one else around. If another man arrives, I first run a check that he is no physical threat— that he is not about to mug me. No one has ever mugged me or hurt me since childhood, but the feeling still lives. (Women understand this reflex, for different reasons.) Then I get to assessing whether he is stronger, has better clothes or is more athletic. If he is with a woman, I look for signs that she doesn't really like him! If the car park is within view, I check out his car for comparison with my own—a good guide to income

and status, as well as taste. Even if he is friendly and a conversation starts, I consider in what light to best present myself (modestly!)—as important and successful. It's really pretty sad, this insecure obsession with comparisons.[4]

Following Biddulph's advice, we are reschooling ourselves. Some of the best days for me (Kim) are hanging out with close friends, unloading about the struggles I am facing and laughing loudly and often without any masks. Some of the best use of my (Darren) time over recent years has been days with two of my best friends: Patrick, who has been a good friend since Bible college and a groomsman at my wedding, and Jason, my brother. When we see one another as allies rather than competitors, we can let our guard down and get the most from our friendships.

We need friends outside our church and mission work, but we value good friendships in our church and mission teams too. We say, "We need you," to people in our churches and teams, not just as a team-building exercise but because we value mutuality in ministry. And we love how church and mission life and our work as pastors and our friendships with fellow travelers overlap. Generations ago pastors were taught, "You can't make close friends with people in your church." We're glad that advice no longer applies.

For Christians, friendship is part of who we are. We are called to follow not just as servants but also as friends with God and with one another. Jesus modeled this for us. He had special friendships, including with two women, Mary and Martha, which was radical in the Greco-Roman world. Someone suggested that Jesus would have breathed a sigh of relief when, after healing, feeding, teaching, answering difficult questions and performing heroic acts of divinity, he was shown simple acts of kindness by Martha, who welcomed him into her home. And her sister Mary listened to him in a way he could trust, with honesty and without expectations (Luke 10:38-39).[5]

The time to cultivate shared life and authentic friendships is before we desperately need them. Crisis time is not a time to develop a supportive relationship; crisis time is when we see the value and the authenticity of the relationships we have.

If you really want to know who your friends are, just make a mistake. When someone makes a large-scale mistake, the tendency is to distance ourselves from him or her. We often are not quite sure what to say or how to respond. But instead of shunning and shaming, we need to grab our friends, draw them close and stand by them. Sharing life may mean a tough talk and a rebuke when needed. But sharing life also means standing by someone as he or she struggles with discerning what to do.

There is a picture of community in Acts 2:42-47 that captures our imagination about sharing life. It impresses us that there are three relationships that are vibrant in this community. First, the church *celebrates* the relationship between God and us: "They worshiped together . . . all the while praising God" (vv. 46-47). They gathered for worship but also worshiped as an everyday community practice. Second, the church *connected* people with one another. They were tight, getting together "each day." Third, the church helped people *contribute* to their world. They "shared everything they had." They were the sort of group that could say, "If you have a genuine need, we'll help you." Community Christian Church, where Kim works, encourages people to be 3C Christ-followers: celebrating in worship, connecting (sharing life) and contributing (through mission).[6]

Because we overestimate what we can achieve as individuals, we reckon we also underestimate what we can achieve together. Margaret Mead, an outspoken American anthropologist, said, "Never doubt that a small group of thoughtful, committed citizens can change the world; indeed, it's the only thing that ever has."[7] Mead captured the imagination of many grassroots organizations that use this as a kind of motto for their sense of community and to reflect their desire to transform the world.

Sometimes people love the idea of community or communal living rather than loving the people God has placed them with. Dietrich Bonhoeffer warned, "[The person] who loves [their] dream of a community more than the Christian community itself becomes a destroyer of the latter, even though [their] personal intentions may be ever so honest."[8] God gives community to us, and gives us to a community. Author Shane Claibornes' paraphrases Bonhoeffer's quote this way: "If you love the vision you have for community, you will destroy community. If you love the people around you, you will create community." We belong where God has sent and placed us. It is no good claiming we love people and the world in general if we neglect to show love to those close to us. Author John Perkins said, "Only God so loved the world. Our responsibility is to love those around us."[9]

CROSS-FERTILIZATION

Tony Wicking, an Anglican minister, came to Forge looking for fresh inspiration for leading his church in missional directions. His church context was fairly traditional. For Tony's church, a decision to move the Communion table is like an act of Congress.

Tony did his residency with Salvation Army officers Troy and Peta Pittaway; their tradition does not practice Communion. While the Anglicans argue over infant baptism, the Salvation Army does not practice baptism at all. They do not have sacraments. So their relationship was like putting Greek and Hebrew together. Their church and ecclesial differences were as black and white as you can get.

But they became friends and learned from one another. Troy and Peta inspired Tony to get involved in addressing homelessness. Tony prayed for Troy and Peta and their ministries. They became fellow journeyers in mission and were inspired by each other.

We are not interested in church as a system that uses people and builds an organization for its own sake. I (Darren) saw enough of that in Europe and saw the deadness of where it leads. Mark and Andrea Michaels, who are developing Forge in Scotland, know traditional church programs will not work, since Scotland is in a post-church era. They are convinced they are called to do one thing with local Scottish people: share life. And they are outstanding at it. The locals love them, and I (Kim) loved meeting every owner of every breakfast joint or coffee house (often followed by some good Scotch whisky at the right time of the day).

People want shared life desperately. When we talk about shared life in churches, in our home cities and around the world, people express a longing for it. Ironically, the ones who want it badly tend to be the worst at it. They move from job and house, marriage and church, looking for something new and forgetting it is themselves they take everywhere. Shared life cannot be something we just consume. It has to be a part of our DNA. Whatever we want to focus on in mission, we want to creatively and authentically worship God. Whenever we want to help one another cultivate genuine spirituality, it has to go hand in hand with sharing life as a community.

7

STANDING IN THE GAP

*But among you it will be different. Those who are the
greatest among you should take the lowest rank,
and the leader should be like a servant.*

JESUS (LUKE 22:26)

*Apostolic ministry calls forth and develops the gifts
and callings of all of God's people. It does not
create reliance but develops the capacities
of the whole people of God based on
the dynamics of the gospel.*

ALAN HIRSCH

THE BLIND SIDE IS A **2009** SPORTS MOVIE about NFL offensive lineman Michael Oher (played by Quinton Arron). "Big
Mike" grew up in foster homes because his mom, a drug addict,
was unable to care for him. A friend's dad regularly gave him a
couch to sleep on and got him into Wingate Christian School on

the promise of his sporting ability. But he was still homeless and struggled with academic work.

Most of the teachers at that Christian school were ready to write him off, but some challenged the school to persevere with Michael. Most significantly, Leigh Anne Tuohy (played by Sandra Bullock) gave him a bed one night, invited him to stay for Thanksgiving and got him some clothes. Over time she did many things, including teaching him how to drive and providing a tutor. Eventually the Tuohys adopted him.

Leigh Anne's belief in Michael and the time she took to understand his strengths helped him develop into an aggressive football player while making the grades to be eligible for a college football scholarship. The movie ends with Michael being selected in the first round of the 2009 NFL draft.

What made the difference for Michael was people—especially Leigh Anne—being willing to stand in the gap for him. And Michael himself stood in the gap for others; he makes his mark in football because of his protective instinct, which causes him to excel at covering his teammates' *blind side*.

Just as Leigh Anne stood in the gap for Michael, and Michael stood in the gap for his teammates, we need people and processes that support and empower us in our sentness. The picture is not complete with just a vision of a new identity of sentness, a commitment to submerge in a neighborhood, a message of fostering shalom. It is not enough to have an innovative idea or a passion for mission. We need those who can stand in the gap for us, and we must stand in the gap for others.

GOOD FOUNDATIONS

Two early communities stood in the gap for me (Kim). I was born in Dandenong, one of poorest cities in the Australian state of Victoria. My mother was a Greek immigrant; she came to Australia in the 1960s on one of many large boats that brought in Egyptians, Italians and Greeks. My mother has had an incredibly hard life. She was put in an Egyptian orphanage as a young child, experienced terrible abuse at the hand of her father and witnessed horrific acts of violence that left her with post-traumatic stress disorder. This mental illness would sometimes debilitate her to the point of exhaustion and hospitalization. Other times she functioned fine, running her own business. When she found herself single and pregnant by a married man, she knew it would bring shame on her family, so she hid the pregnancy until birth.

I never met my biological father, nor do I have any memories of the man who married my mother when I was four, even though he adopted me and gave me his surname. I know he loved me; my sister tells me she's sure he still does. It feels like a lifetime ago.

I am told we traveled a lot, living in hotels that he and my mother managed, which consisted of a pub, accommodations and a restaurant. I do remember some of the places we lived in for brief periods, but I don't have a single memory of him as my father. My lack of memory could be due to the fact that in the middle of the night, when I was nine, he got up, took our car and left me with a distraught mother and crying baby sister, four years my junior. I remember my mother waking me early in the morning, saying, "Dad is gone." She was crying uncontrollably, and I had to open the General Store we ran at the front of our house.

My mother met and later married my third father, her second husband, in my early teen years. I loved Rick like a dad and took his name. He was good to me, and for the first time I felt I had a whole family. His sons and daughters became my brothers and sisters—for a little while. I still have a great affection for some of them and still keep in contact a bit. As we moved around from house to house, however, Mom's illness would cause her to lash out abusively sometimes. I never doubted her love; she read me the

Bible and seeded in me a love and fear of God. But I often experienced her brokenness and a life of trauma.

The miracle for me was that a lifelong friend of her and her husband paid for my sister and me to go to Maranatha Christian School, which would be one of two discipling communities I experienced as a teenager. I joined the school's Christian drama team and was given the chance to introduce dramas and to speak in front of hundreds of young people at public schools at the ages of twelve and thirteen. While things were completely crazy at home, I knew I could go to school and find adults who would stand in the gap and care for, invest in and affirm me.

I loved being a part of the drama team, which was called "Shatter The Darkness." We had STD printed on our shirts and never thought for a second why others yelled out rude things. We didn't care; we were a team communicating Jesus through drama in brave ways. I learned to perform under pressure and persecution. I also grew into leadership roles and was given a number of public speaking opportunities. I was school captain and a senator from year ten to graduation at the end of year twelve.

The teachers at Maranatha became surrogate parents as they watched me in plays and other performances over the years. If there was an excursion or extracurricular activity, teachers took me aside and asked me if I needed help to cover any costs. They often paid those costs themselves. They also gave me plenty of opportunities to grow, helping me through rebukes and corrections to my character (or lack thereof). I know today a good portion of who I am as a father, pastor, preacher and person is largely because of this discipling community that stood in the gap for me.

The second community I experienced was my local church, South Eastern Christian Centre. Steve Swain stood in the gap for me as my youth pastor right in the middle of my mom marrying for the second time and Rick becoming my third father. Without Maranatha and the Swains, I would never have had a context for understanding lifelong discipleship, shared life and community.

THE HEART OF AN OLD JEW

We love the heart of an old Jew who prayed, "O God, you have taught me from my earliest childhood, and I constantly tell others about the wonderful things you do. Now that I am old and gray, do not abandon me, O God. Let me proclaim your power to this new generation, your mighty miracles to all who come after me" (Psalm 71:17-18). Does that reflect your heart? Do you want to stand in the gap for the next generation? Do you want to help people's imaginations be captured by a cause that is greater than them?

King David, who wrote this psalm, is a great example of someone who heard the call to follow God as a young person and served until he was old. He did not have a trouble-free life. He did not have a spotless record. But as he increased in years and his health declined, he still sought God, and he sought to stand in the gap for the next generation so they could understand God's purposes.

We need Davids in our lives who will stand in the gap for us. Younger people need older people. Young leaders need experienced leaders. Leaders with dreams need champions for those dreams. Missionary apprentices need experienced missionaries who will teach them what they have learned, believe in them, care for them, share hope with them, listen to them, spark their imaginations and challenge them to give an experiment a go. As we engage in risky mission, we need experienced players who will coach us to go for greater things than we think possible. We need older folks who can see our gifts.

Young people have expressed frustration that they don't know what they do well. They say they would love having someone older in the faith who could say, "Hey, I've noticed you do this well" or "Have you thought about serving God in this area?" or "Why don't you give your idea a go? And by the way, how can I help?"

Just as younger people need older people's sponsorship, older people need younger people with their visions, daring boldness and criticism of hypocrisy. So if you classify yourself as older, be encouraged to welcome the contribution and innovation of young people. And those who are younger, be encouraged to learn from, lean on and value the traditions and innovations of older generations.

It is unfortunate when young people are not given a voice in organizational culture in the church. We need their voice and vision and wisdom. But it is equally unfortunate when older people are sidelined by a youth-obsessed culture. We need their voice and wisdom and vision. Younger and older generations each have a responsibility to stand in the gap for the other. Joel 2:28 celebrates a future when old people will dream dreams and young people will see visions. There is a generation gap, but in that there is value, because each generation has a contribution to make. Generation gaps in our society and churches are something to celebrate, not bemoan. But we need to stand for one another across those gaps.[1]

I (Darren) really appreciated older Christians taking an interest in me: my dad, my first boss, my Bible college vice principal, an elder in my first church, the church secretary who prayed with me every week, my research supervisor and others who have sponsored me in ministry opportunities.

Howard Smith, the elder in my first church, took me aside when I was a new youth pastor and told me, "You can do it. You're not alone. And I believe in you." While I was cowriting this book, my research supervisor, Ross Langmead, caught a train to encourage me over coffee. If you see a young leader with potential, tell him or her. When you encounter lonely people, young or old, befriend them. If you know of young people with self-esteem hassles or challenges to their self-confidence, build them up. They need your wisdom, even when they think they know it all. They need you to believe in them, especially if they don't believe in themselves. They need you to trust them, even if they have betrayed your trust in the past. And they need to hear about values, even if they think they're old-fashioned. They also need to hear your vision for the future, even if they do not have much hope. And mostly they need your example.

SOME OF OUR BEST FRIENDS

This kind of empowering leadership and standing in the gap is important between generations. It is also important for people of other cultures and other minorities, including women.

When we ignore the gifts of women or relegate them to particular roles, we limit the capacity of our churches to live out the fullness of our shared mission. As men, we both appreciate learning from and being inspired by our sisters and daughters in the church. Some of our best friends are women. Some of the best leaders and missionaries we know are women.

There is no gender discrimination in our understanding of sentness. Unfortunately, the voices of women are not always heard in our churches—and missional churches are not the exception in this. Ultimately the world needs women whom the church believes in and commissions to do their mission in the world. We need to stand in the gap for women and their leadership contribution.

We also need to stand in the gap for our sisters and brothers from different cultures. In terms of both numbers and passion, the global church is becoming less Western and more Asian, Latin and African. Western countries are also becoming more culturally diverse, which challenges those of us who are white or Anglo not just to be hospitable to people from other cultures but to welcome them onto worship, leadership and pastoral teams.

Cultural diversity brings complexity and communication challenges. People of different cultures expect to worship and make decisions in different ways. But this can add richness. We can learn more about God when we read the Bible together from our different cultural perspectives than if we worship only with people like us.

As I (Kim) was taking the role of director of Forge International, I asked our team if we could create a scorecard to measure how we were doing. I was not just looking to measure new hubs and new staff; I wanted us to be asking one another some questions:

- How diverse are we? Are we only white or are we being inclusive of others?

- How much equality do we express? Are men and women given equal opportunities?

- Are we creating an unleadership culture? Do we push power to the margins?

I (Darren) have learned much about multicultural ministry from my colleague and friend Robyn Song. She was born in Korea but grew up in Australia as the daughter of a Korean church pastor. Robyn has exercised leadership roles in Korean and multicultural churches, and came to Auburn as an intern to help lead us in more vibrant and relevant multicultural ministry. Robyn now coordinates our Auburn hub for international students and is leading a team that offers English teaching, hospitality and Bible study.

One of Robyn's best contributions to the church is helping us understand what it takes to be a church that is hospitable and welcoming to people of different cultures. We want non-Westerners not just to be welcome as visitors but also to be included as equals. We want to connect with international students, as we have started to do, but also connect better with the greater-than-average Chinese and Indian populations in our neighborhood. We want to partner with other culturally diverse congregations with whom we might not only share worship space but also cooperate in shared mission and worship. Robyn's voice is invaluable as we grapple with these ministry issues.

In our church tribes, some of the most inspiring people are from different cultural backgrounds. We are in awe of the faith and perseverance of Karen and Chin, refugees from Burma who have much to teach us about faith in the face of suffering. We want to learn from Christians in Asia who have lived in the midst of religious pluralism for many generations. We are inspired by Korean Christians with their commitment to prayer and global mission. Our openness to God is focused as we hear testimony of Muslim-background believers from the Middle East and their experiences of God through dreams and prayer. When we talk about shared life, the communal perspectives of most non-Western cultures challenge our blatant individualism.

LEADERSHIP SUCCESSION

The best leaders make decisions based not on how it will affect them and their church now, but on the difference it will make for the next generation.

We have already referred briefly to an inspiring example of a pastor standing in the gap for a next-generation leader. At Urban Life, Doug Faircloth had been youth pastor for five years and then senior pastor for fourteen years when God had challenged him with a subversive question: "If the only joy I give you in ministry is the joy or sense of fulfillment you get from what your sons and daughters do, is it enough for you?" Doug empowered a young team of leaders to imagine with him radically new directions for the church. One of the leaders was Anthea Smits, whom he had appointed to the leadership team when she was twenty-five. He began grooming her for the call to leadership that the team discerned she had. As the church moved and changed its name, Doug took the plunge and handed senior leadership over to Anthea.

Innovation does not happen in a vacuum; it needs a permission-giving and empowering culture. Doug fostered that in his church and among emerging leaders through his mentoring and sponsorship of them. After handing over leadership, at Anthea's invitation he stayed on part time as coaching pastor for the team. Anthea honors Doug for his vision of transformation and the confidence he showed in them as young adults who had grown up in his youth group, and she continues to describe Doug as their "voice of wisdom." Doug modeled empowering leadership for Anthea, and she is explicit about her sense of responsibility to empower others.[2] Encouraging sentness requires innovators who can propose ideas and pioneer new initiatives, but it also requires sponsors who can stand in the gap for them.

DANCING WITH YOUR LEADERS

A pastor was driving behind one of his deacons after a meeting. The deacon had forgotten something and did a sudden U-turn, causing a head-on collision with the pastor. Miraculously they survived without a scratch. The deacon said, "Praise God, we should put our disagreements behind us. This is obviously a sign from God of his care. I know you don't usually drink, but let's have one to celebrate our new relationship."

"Drink what?" the pastor asked.

The deacon held out a bottle and replied, "How about the scotch I was keeping for a special occasion? Have a swig."

The pastor had a long gulp—quite a long gulp. The deacon screwed the lid back on the bottle and threw it into the river.

"Aren't you going to have a drink?" the pastor asked.

The deacon replied, "No, the police will be here any minute . . . with a breathalyzer."

We don't know whether you find that joke funny or not, but it is an illustration of the things we can do to one another to get ahead, to make our point or to make *us* look better.

One thing we have learned in the churches we have pastored is that fruitful leadership and church health have as much, or more, to do with trust and good relationships between pastor and church as a host of other factors, including whether the pastor is exceptionally gifted or the church especially healthy. It is not about the contract between us but the dance we develop. It breaks our heart to see churches struggling with hope and vision, and colleagues in ministry whose enthusiasm is deflated and good-heartedness soured, because they may have the contract in place but haven't learned how to dance together.

Once, at a wedding reception, I (Darren) picked up a dance with a friend next to me. But I was a little too enthusiastic and trod on her toes. I didn't get with the rhythm. I have had that experience with churches sometimes too. What is it that keeps us from dancing well together?

Ministry and congregational life are more an art form than a science. As a pastor and a congregation come together, there are certain employment arrangements involved. But the far more critical aspect of the relationship is not captured by employment arrangements, salary figures or bank accounts. The ministry-making or ministry-breaking elements for a pastor in a church have much more to do with relationships and trust.

I (Darren) worked several years ago with a leadership team that wanted to express their expectations of each other and the hopes for their teamwork. So they drafted a covenant that included things like supporting one another, working together collaboratively, exercising open communication and courteous disagreement, maintaining confidentiality and encouraging critical people to speak to the people they are criticizing. It was a helpful exercise to talk about expectations and a helpful framework to refer to. We need to be doing life together and sharing in a sense of mission. But we also need to commit ourselves to standing in the gap for one another.

Whatever team you work in and whatever other commitments

you make to one another, one key element is essential in healthy and loving relationships. That key ingredient is mutual encouragement. In 1 Thessalonians, the apostle Paul recognizes that the world can be an unfriendly place. It is easy to get hurt. At times we are surrounded by frustrating circumstances and people. With the hope of God's dream for a better world, Paul says to the Thessalonians, "So encourage each other and build each other up, just as you are already doing" (1 Thessalonians 5:11). Encouragement is not something we leave to those who are gifted in it or to paid professionals. We all need encouragement, and it is up to all of us to offer it.

We highly value the encouragement we have received from different people in all the churches we have served. That has come in prayer when our families were struggling, in care when we were sick, in nurture and interest in our children, in hospitality that went both ways and in shared fun. We give our all to the mission of our churches, whether reciprocity is there or not, but it makes it a whole lot more life giving and sustainable when ministry goes both ways.

I (Darren) am thankful for an encouraging and permission-giving church at Auburn Life. I feel a strong sense of encouragement from many people in the church, across their diverse ages, cultures, backgrounds and histories. A third of the church was there before we came. Their openness to explore new directions and to affirm my ministry has been very encouraging—and a credit to them. Another third came to the church when we were called, inspired by a vision to grow a vibrant, multicultural, mission-shaped community. They have been gracious to those who have been there longer and have willingly taken on leadership responsibilities alongside the older leaders. Yet another third has joined us in the past few years and picked up on the ethos of mutual encouragement. We have made some changes, with people's generous permission. We have changed the direction we face in church, hung art on the walls, brought in lounge chairs and retired hymnbooks to the cupboard. More significantly, we have appointed three interns and started a hub for international students. Those changes made some people uncomfortable, but they have endorsed them for the future of the church.

In one process, we were able to change the whole constitution with a small committee that met over a few weeks and then a ten-minute church meeting. Contrast that with another church where I tried to make one constitutional change: the church took a year to consider it—and said no.

When you are leading, be empowering and give permission to your teams. When you are following, it is just as important to be encouraging and supportive to your leaders.

Dreaming at Solace

Solace, profiled earlier in the book, is a church that functions as a network standing in the gap for people, empowering their everyday spirituality and mission.[3] They have experimented with alternative worship and run a thrift shop and other community ministries, but their foundational drive is to help people reflect on their passions and dreams and become better neighbors, friends, advocates and representatives of the kingdom of God wherever in the world they find themselves. Solace is not interested in just recruiting people to fill church positions but wants to uphold the bigger vision of empowering people to remake their world.

Solace's founding leader, Olivia Maclean, coached Kate in her community group involvement. Having suffered pelvic instability during a pregnancy, Kate realized there were no support groups and little information available about the condition. So she and five other women started the Pelvic Instability Association to support those suffering from it and to educate the public—including medical professionals, who often misdiagnose it.

As Kate was starting the association, the Solace Leadership Team (SLT) tried to recruit her, but when they found out what she was doing, they withdrew their invitation and sought instead to support her with her group. Olivia wanted to help Kate with her work for God in the world, not just recruit her to run what Olivia is in charge of under a Solace banner.

Dreaming Nights are a service sponsored by Solace to help individuals and groups who are yearning to change the places where they live and work. These nights are designed foster questions and encourage plans to balance spirituality and concerns for justice. People can get assistance with the development of a business plan, applying for seed funding or whatever else is needed to help make a dream a reality. Solace has tossed around ideas about what a partner church can do with their manse, including letting it out for free to young adults who commit to some form of incarnational mission and intentional community. One leader has a vision for a health center with a Jesus-centered spirituality. And a group asked for help raising $10,000 for Opportunity International.

Solace also stands in the gap for the local neighborhood and encourages people to dream imaginatively for neighborhood transformation. The group is now based in a storefront community space in Alphington, but when they were meeting at St. Paul's Anglican Church Fairfield, they formed a collaborative group to explore how they could develop their space and engage their broader community. The dreaming group was called SPACE, or SPACEmakers, suggestive of both the partnership between St. Paul's (SP) and Solace (ACE) and their shared hope for making community-friendly spaces.

They pooled their resources and ideas, involving eight people from St. Paul's and Solace and an employed project manager. Their task was to explore how best to develop their facilities and engage with their busy shopping street. They broadened their agenda and used their regular meetings to discern what they could see God doing in their community. In the first hour of every SPACEmakers meeting, they sought to be attentive and to discuss these topics for discernment:

- Things to cheer
- Changes to be a part of
- Crisis/conflict in which to be a peacemaker
- Celebrations to join in
- Crowds or coincidences to pay attention to
- Conversations that lead somewhere

They also discussed building redevelopment implications and financing options, but they wanted to ensure they were focusing on openness to the community rather than becoming building centered. That partnership did not ultimately happen, but Solace has continued to use similar community development principles and offer Christian spirituality resources to their adopted neighborhood.

Solace seeks to nurture the freedom to dream and to foster the kingdom of God in their everyday worlds. The leaders do not see their role as "doing" ministry, but as imparting the ethos of Solace and standing in the gap for others, helping them remake the world in line with God's dream. Solace leaders are at their best when they are championing innovation in others. Their basic pastoral toolkit is not so much the therapeutic "How are you feeling?" as much as exploratory coaching: "What are you passionate about?" and "How is God calling you to participate in remaking the world?"[4]

The biggest challenge of sentness is not what we *do* in church, but how we *be* church in the world—and we need leaders who stand in the gap for their people to help them express their faith not just in "Sunday stuff" but in remaking the world beyond the confines of the church sanctuary.

LOWERING THE BAR

Sometimes we need to lower our expectations for what being the church *gathered* involves and increase our aspirations for how God's people can be the church when they are *scattered* in the world. We love the way Neil Cole urges missional Christians to lower the bar on how we do church and raise the bar on discipleship. He is a hero of ours because of his simple evangelism and his disciple-making and church-planting principles.

Churches use all sorts of ways to attract people, especially with Sunday services. Cole suggests taking Jesus to people, rather than waiting for them to come to us. He has used this approach to start hundreds of "organic churches." It is not that Cole does not have a high view of church—he loves and celebrates the church. But he bemoans that the understanding of church that most followers of Jesus have makes it hard for them to express their faith in everyday life. When he was planting his first church, his team wanted to set up a coffee shop, but instead they felt led to existing coffee shops where lost people already were. Cole urges planting seeds of the kingdom of God where life happens and society is formed: coffee shops, schools, homes, restaurants, neighborhoods, campuses and workplaces.

The vision of organic church is "Every Christian is a church planter, every home is a church, and every church building is a training center." Cole stands in the gap for ordinary believers being church in everyday places, declaring hopefully, "I believe we are leaving the day of the ordained and ushering in the day of the ordinary. It is a time when common Christians will do uncommon deeds."[5]

Organic approaches to church and leadership are not just for newly planted, grassroots-style, "simple" churches. Cole and his cofounder of Church Multiplication Associates, Phil Helfer, have a vision for thousands of new simple churches but also thousands of churches changed organically and refocused on disciple making. This is not primarily about making churches more attractive but about empowering missional Christians to grow their faith and let it spill out on the streets. The kind of leadership that is needed for revitalization is one that stands in the gap. According to Cole and Hefler, leadership does not start with grand vision statements but with acknowledging dependence on God and standing in the gap to invite people to humbly listen and to be attentive to what God is doing. It is not about delivering ideal vision and strategic agendas, but giving people permission to dream imaginatively and follow Jesus fruitfully.

Some engineering and business groups develop "skunk works," which are tasked with developing creative options without having to work within traditional institutional expectations. The best church leaders pour energy into creative options and champion pioneering leaders who can explore out-of-the-box possibilities and ask, "Why not?" Innovators in our churches are few and far between, and they need leaders who can stand in the gap for them. Cole and Helfer urge leaders to give permission for new ideas, innovate new ministries beyond the walls of the church building, create boundaries only when necessary and block criticism for those who are giving something new a go.

As new life emerges, leaders celebrate others' stories. This does not take a high level of management—in fact, the best approach to leadership is not to overmanage but to trust that Jesus is guiding the church into fresh expressions of mission.[6]

Part of the obstacle to standing in the gap for the mission of the whole people of God is that the way we imagine church, with clergy employed for ministry, causes us to rely too much on hired holy people. Even in churches with intentional leadership development and internship programs, sometimes the focus is on recruiting for professional church ministry. But empowerment is needed not just for interns and staff, and not just to release people into ministry projects in a church. We have heard young adults working in their professions express disquiet that a lot of focus and effort goes into extracting people from the workplace, while little effort is given to helping people in the workplace integrate faith and professional life. We also have heard Christians say they love their hobbies or sports and want to integrate that love with their love of God. Unfortunately, often a sport or hobby is seen as a competitor with church rather than as part of a holistic expression of faith.

All people of God need empowerment for thinking about mission in their weekday lives. When a church can grasp the vision that it is the role of followers of Jesus to engage in mission and that it is the role of leaders to stand in the gap and empower them to do that, it unleashes enormous potential.

CONTENTION BETWEEN DISCIPLES

Jesus called and empowered twelve disciples to learn and do the same things he was doing—bring healing and wholeness, teach about God's offer of forgiveness and interest in all people, and set people free from what binds them. The Gospels deal with these episodes of Jesus' modeling, as he taught the disciples by example. Sometimes they got it wrong, but there was then a lesson to learn. Just because something does not work out, that does not mean it was not worth doing and learning from.

One day the disciples heard about someone else doing what they were doing—driving out demons—but in another place and context, unsanctioned and outside the official membership of the Twelve. They became anxious and concerned, perhaps on Jesus' behalf or perhaps because it was not them in the limelight.

> John said to Jesus, "Teacher, we saw someone using your name to cast out demons, but we told him to stop because he wasn't in our group."
>
> "Don't stop him!" Jesus said. "No one who performs a miracle in my name will soon be able to speak evil of me. Anyone who is not against us is for us. If anyone gives you even a cup of water because you belong to the Messiah, I tell you the truth, that person will surely be rewarded." (Mark 9:38-41)

Perhaps it is human nature to try to keep the opportunity for doing good to ourselves. When others use *our* idea to accomplish the same thing and they get the credit, we tend to feel ripped off. If they are "not one of us," why should they be able to use our good idea? Shouldn't we get at least some of the credit?

But Jesus has a different perspective. Counterculturally, he implies that if good is happening, who gets the credit doesn't matter. (In fact the miracles in this episode are done in Jesus' name anyway, so credit is going to the right place, even if the disciples are left out.) The most important thing is that our service is done in Jesus' name. It is not about the messenger but about the message, not about the channel but about the source of life. Jesus reminds us to celebrate that good is being done in his name, whoever does it. And maybe we can learn something from other groups who are doing good in different ways.

PARLEY AND FRESH EXPRESSIONS

Different expressions of church sometimes distrust or question what other expressions are doing. It's human nature. But that part of human nature is called pride.

For us, a vision of sentness is not about pride in a particular style of church. You might prefer megachurch or house church, Hillsong or hymns, and still live a life of sentness. We encourage all different streams of church life to learn from one another.

Stuart Murray is a champion for new expressions of church and an advocate for fresh and inherited expressions of churches learning from and leaning on one another. Murray urges us to be prepared to parley (language borrowed from pirates, as demonstrated in the *Pirates of the Caribbean* movies) with one another, engaging in conversation and mutual learning. Existing churches can be inspired by the creativity and fresh efforts of diverse new groups—those reconfiguring around community, reimagining worship or reshaping around mission. But many of these new communities need existing inherited forms of church to stand in the gap for them with permission, resources and coaching out of their experience.[7]

We all have things we still need to learn. Sometimes people from other groups help us see our weak areas. But it is sad when one group feels the need to put another down to feel superior. We do not need to say, "Someone else is doing church in our street, and we tried to stop them because they are not one of us" or "Someone else is saying they are missional, but they are not one of us." We don't want to lose the meaning of what missional is or have it watered down, but let's champion what God is doing missionally in all different contexts.

The book *Mission-Shaped Church: Church Planting and Fresh Expressions of Church in a Changing Context*, which we use as one of our textbooks for our Forge residents, was seminal in identifying the potential for innovative experiments in the Church of England.[8] It includes a good example of a denominational system giving license to cultivating missional imagination. It advocates a "mixed economy" strategy of planting new congregations as part of and alongside revitalizing existing congregations. It challenges existing churches to give permission for dreaming and experimenting with new initiatives and facilitating them with resources and partnership. And it encourages fresh expressions of church to work in collaboration with inherited churches.

This was a bold move in the Anglican Church, which has traditionally followed a parish system, where each church has responsibility for pastoral care and mission in their parish. It is unusual to plant an Anglican church in another church's area. But the world has changed. Fresh expressions assumes we need new churches to reach different kinds of people and to connect with networks of people from across different parishes.

Examples of fresh expressions include network-based churches that may not meet on Sundays or keep to parish boundaries.

Churches may also focus on a particular subgroup of people rather than a geographic area. The movement has birthed café churches, cell churches, base ecclesial communities, alternative worship services, seeker gatherings, new monastic groups, youth congregations and school-linked, midweek community development. And those in denominational and leadership training systems have sought to cooperate with those exploring new approaches, and have aimed to identify, train and credential pioneer leaders.

PERMISSION-GIVING EMPOWERMENT

There is a gravitational pull on established churches that have not yet embraced *missio Dei*, or whose missionary zeal has been either exoticized (relegated only to those who follow Jesus to the other side of the world) or domesticated by the day-to-day demands of an established organization and the allure of the consumer culture whose air they breathe. Yet a missionary movement that embraces *missio Dei* is intuitively attractive to followers of Jesus, wherever they are, because Jesus is a missionary God calling us on his mission.

There are people in every local church looking for someone to give language and license to their intuitive longings for a more dynamic discipleship. Meanwhile, missionary movements need a fixed point to reflect on, a history with lessons learned to be drawn from and resources—or even an endowment to invest in God's missionary work. We need each other.

Creative initiatives often start with a leader's vision for something new, as well as an invitation to others to join in out-of-the-box brainstorming and dreaming. Good church planters have a thought-through approach to developing ministries and usually some idea of the shape of the church they are planting, but they are also eager to involve and empower others in their teams to dream and plan alongside them.

We love hearing from people who feel empowered by their leaders. We love hearing about pastors who ask their people, "What is capturing your imagination? What is touching your heart about the needs of our community and world? What dreams do you have? How can we help you fulfill them?"

At Forge we encourage outside-the-box thinking and give-it-a-go action. When it comes to experimentation, it does not matter if you fail. It is better to succeed. But failure is better than not trying new things. Programs, preoccupations and theories might hold people back from pioneering new things, but Forge encourages them to tread into uncharted areas. We strive to give people permission when their churches or organizations, peer groups or their own imaginations might have limited and restricted them.

When people's toolkits are limited to certain tools, they need imagination. If you only know how to use a hammer, you see everything as a nail. We give people permission to imagine and try different tools and approaches.

We love local churches, but we also want leaders to be able to imagine and develop all sorts of new expressions of local churches and mission. That's why we invite practitioners to come and share their stories of innovative mission—not so that Forge residents will copy and imitate them, but so they will be inspired to imagine similarly creative innovation for their contexts. That's why we allocate practitioner coaches to residents—so someone can encourage and help them put their dreams into action. That's why creative types find Forge a breeding ground for connecting their art with their mission. The purist and the nonconformist both find a place in our training. We stand in the gap for the radical and the poet, the artist and the activist, the pastor and the prophet. We encourage you to foster the same sort of culture in your church and your community.

Sometimes people just need someone who will stand in the gap and give them a go-ahead. Susan Boyle is one of the most famous contestants on *Britain's Got Talent*. She volunteered at her local church and always loved to sing. So she lined up with thousands of other hopefuls in 2009 to let Britain and the world know of her skill. When the judges asked her what she wanted to get out of the show, she replied, "I want to be a professional musician."

Now, you need to understand that Susan did not look like a likely candidate for singing at the bar, let alone on a stage. She was forty-seven years old—twice as old as most of the contestants. People snickered and raised their eyebrows—until she sang her first line. She blew the judges and the audience away with her confident and heartfelt rendition of a *Les Misérables* song, "I Dreamed a Dream."[9]

We want to say, "The church's got talent." Our churches need to be full of talent scouts who are watching for people's giftedness and how they can make a difference and embrace their sentness in the world.

CONCLUSION

Starting Something New

For I am about to do something new.
See, I have already begun! Do you not see it?
I will make a pathway through the wilderness.
I will create rivers in the dry wasteland.

ISAIAH 43:19

Planting a new church, or remissionalizing an existing one,
in this approach isn't primarily about buildings, worship services,
size of congregations, and pastoral care, but rather about gearing the
whole community around natural discipling friendships, worship
as lifestyle, and mission in the context of everyday life. As a
living network "in Christ" it can meet anywhere, anytime
and still be a viable expression of church. This is a
much more organic way to plant a church
or to revitalize it.

ALAN HIRSCH AND DARRYN ALTCLASS

I (Kim) am a terrible handyman. Something breaks at my house, and we throw it out. Early in our marriage we were living in a bungalow, and I noticed three lightbulbs were out. So I got a stool, climbed up and balanced up there on that stool. That's difficult for a guy as big as me. I unscrewed the first blown bulb, and I noticed it had a turning thing on the end. You screw it in and out. So I took note of what I needed to get to replace it and stuck it in my pocket. The second one did not screw out, but turned and unlocked with a Frankenstein thing on the end. The third socket did not have a bulb in it. I was not sure whether it was a screw-in or Franken-stein-end bulb. So I stuck my finger in to test which kind it was.

When I woke up, I was in the Christmas tree, with my feet poking out of it. I looked at my finger, and it was on fire. That was not a good sign. It was glowing and hot, like I was ET trying to phone home. Then I smelled smoke and realized my hair was on fire. So I tried to put out my hair with the hand that included the burning finger. Not a good idea. That whole episode was not my finest hour.

We like dangerous stories of people doing risky things—but not the "put your finger in the socket and see what happens" kind of risky. We encourage you to take risks to advance the kingdom of God—that is, to start something new that reflects your particular sentness. Risks like that may be costly, but they aren't risky, because they're at the heart of what it means to be a follower of Jesus.

We come to church on Sundays because we need the community of God's people. The Bible encourages us to gather and pray, listen to the Bible and encourage one another. But true community does not come from an hour staring at the backs of other people's heads. Community is more than a Bible study and a church service. And God's call on our lives is more than attending a Sunday show and listening to someone chat. God's call is to serve God in the world. We need the gathering of church to empower us for that.

Gathering isn't exclusive to a consumer church; a sent church also gathers. But let's avoid being content with church as just gathering. Even a gathering is a dangerous story of sentness.

SECRET SAUCE OF THE MISSIONAL TRIBE

A number of groups are jumping on the missional bandwagon. Rather than name and bash anybody, we want to simply say there is a way to see who is taking the missional incarnational theology seriously: they start new things. It's not just a conversation or a conference. It's not just a blog or books about how the church needs to change.

Someone said the emerging church is like sex in junior high. A lot of kids might be talking about it, but not a lot of them are actually doing it. Those that are can get pretty messy and are as fertile as anything.[1] If you are serious about mission, we encourage you to take the risk of starting something new. Don't just seek to change the church. If you want to change the church, that's good, but it's just second base. We need to go to second base, but we don't want to park there forever. Don't just seek to change the church; dream about going all the way and changing the world.

We wish we could introduce you face to face to those who have inspired us with their dangerous stories. Among them are Ruth Hairston and Kate Taylor.

Responding to the challenge to foster missional imagination and practice, Ruth and Colin Hairston and their children sold everything they owned. I (Kim) was there as their kids watched their TV being carried away. They packed enough clothes to carry on their backs and moved to Thailand.

Wanting to help the Karen refugees, who were fleeing Burma into Thailand, they set up as a family near the Thai-Burma boarder and began inspiring, training and equipping local leaders. Together they marched into the jungle and set up a school and home for students.

Ruth is an exceptional missionary. She went through a Forge residency, planted two churches in Australia and, with the same conviction and purpose, started a not-for-profit community development agency called Connect3e. When a young Thai mom came and begged them to adopt her baby, Ruth and Colin and their four children opened their arms to little Tate. Ruth has planted churches, started not-for-profits and changed the lives of hundreds of displaced refugees. She does it all while treating the Karen people with dignity and grace.

People like Ruth inspire us. Ruth demonstrates what it is to be a servant to the people she is sent to with her family.

Like Ruth, Kate Taylor is a mom, with three boys. In 1999 she went to Cambodia for a mission trip. What was to follow was one of the most courageous acts we know of. When she came back from her trip, Kate went back to school to become a midwife nurse. She then started the 2h Project, which has set up a farm, a microenterprise loan scheme and a series of medical clinics, for which Kate received a special commendation from the king of Thailand. Today hundreds of people go to Cambodia on medical mercy trips organized by 2h and led by local leaders.

We know these families personally. We know neither of them sought fame or fortune; they have launched and funded both of these not-for-profits out of their own pockets. So don't tell us moms can't change the world. Don't tell us mechanics can't change the world. Don't tell us God is not wooing people to himself.

Ruth and Kate saw God at work and joined him. In the same way, don't wait for God to crash into your world; look for the signs and join in with what God is doing. That is where the blessing is. Don't look for what doors God might open in ten years. Look around you now, and see where your passion overlaps with the needs of the world.

Frederick Buechner says your vocation is "the place where your deep gladness and the world's deep hunger meet."[2] What are you passionate about where the world needs some significant transformation? Be encouraged to start something new and participate in the mission of God—not just in consuming church.

BURSTING WINESKINS

Jesus copped criticism from the religious Pharisees, which you can expect, but also from his own family and friends. Matthew tells us that one action-packed day, after the exhilaration of forgiving and healing a paralytic man and calling and partying with Matthew and his colorful friends, Jesus was challenged by disciples of John the Baptist—one of his best friends: "Why don't your disciples fast like we do and the Pharisees do?" (Matthew 9:14). Did you ever get sick of being criticized for table manners when you were young? Jesus was surely getting tired of criticism about his eating habits.

John the Baptist had taught his followers the important and helpful spiritual discipline of fasting. They went without food so they could focus on prayer and build their spiritual muscles of self-denial. It is a good discipline, and they had learned it well. They would easily win on a competition like *Survivor*. And their spiritual capacities were well developed. But like anyone on to a good thing, they mistakenly thought everyone should follow God their way. When they saw Jesus and his disciples fasting so little and eating so much, and enjoying it, they wanted to know why they were missing out.

Whatever the motive for the question, Jesus' answer is instructive:

Jesus responded "Should the wedding guests mourn while celebrating with the groom? Someday he will be taken from them, and then they will fast. And who would patch an old garment with unshrunk cloth? For the patch shrinks and pulls away from the old cloth, leaving an even bigger hole than before. And no one puts new wine into old wineskins. The old skins would burst from the pressure, spilling the wine and ruining the skins. New wine must be stored in new wine-skins. That way both the wine and the wineskins are pre-served." (Matthew 9:15-17)

For Jesus' followers, there would be a time when fasting and absti-nence would be more appropriate. But while Jesus was with them, it was more fitting to focus on eating with the people Jesus loved. Eating and hospitality were just as much spiritual exercises as fasting and abstinence. But Jesus' imagination was not filled with spiritual exercises for their own sake, but exercises that connected him with the mission of God.

To invite his listeners to capture this alternative imagination, Jesus introduced two illustrations about clothing and wine. Most people in the Western world throw out old clothes rather than repair them. But those who sew know that there is an art to repairing clothes. It is not good practice to sew new patches on old material. The old material has already changed shape and fixed in place. Any newly attached material will change shape when washed, so it can rip the original material. I (Darren) once had one of my wife's old sweaters expanded to fit me. But when we washed it, it shrank to fit our ten-year-old daughter, Emily. If Emily tears it on the trampoline, we are not going to patch it with new cloth and wash it again.

Similarly, when new wine is put into a skin to mature, the skin swells and expands. Old wineskins have already swelled and ex-panded, however; they are no longer flexible, so the skin might burst with the change, and then the skin is ruined and the wine lost. New wine needs new wineskins.

Like patches and wineskins, new moves of God, Jesus implies, need new forms and frameworks to make the most of them. Jesus' lesson inspires us to ask what new patches and wineskins God might be calling us to imagine. And how can we empower a new generation of out-of-the-box practitioners to start something new?

EINSTEIN AND GODLY IMAGINATION

Besides being easily the greatest scientist of the twentieth century, Albert Einstein was a genius at lateral thinking and a champion of imagination. His thoughts encourage us to utilize imagination as a necessary resource for mission:

> I am enough of an artist to draw freely upon my imagination. Imagination is more important than knowledge. Knowledge is limited. Imagination encircles the world.
>
> If you can't imagine it, you can't do it.
>
> The kind of thinking that will solve the world's problems will be of a different order to the kind of thinking that created them in the first place.[3]

Einstein had the twentieth century's greatest scientific mind. As a theoretical physicist, he is widely known for his paradigm-changing scientific theories. But he could see the world in new ways because of his capacity for imagination.

We are convinced that the church in the West needs to foster a distinctly missional imagination. That is what we give our energy to as pastors and as trainers, and it's why we are writing this book together. In grappling with what it means to be a missional church, there are ideas to learn, but far more important is the place of imagination. Mike Frost and Alan Hirsch quote Einstein and appeal to churches to *imagine* that we could do church in different ways, to take risks and experiment like mad. The world is changing around us. The church needs to do whatever it takes, within the ethical bounds of the gospel, to make Christ known to our changing world. We need new wine, and we need new wineskins.

Bono, lead singer for U2, challenges people to "dream up the world you want to live in. Dream out loud, at high volume." The church's role is to help people dream big about how God wants to transform our world. It gives a new position description to our role as pastors, teachers, denominational resource people, trainers of missionaries and change agents. Just as "in every seed there is a forest," when we look at the people in our churches and the churches in our networks, we can see thousands of missionaries in waiting and hundreds of pregnant church-planting organisms. Let's explore in what directions their creative energies are flowing. Let's keep asking believers, leaders, churches and denominations, "What would it look like for you to incarnate the gospel where you live and work?"[4] What about you? What new thing could you start?

IT'S NOT THAT HARD

Hearing stories of incarnational mission is dangerous for your life plans. For us, the experience over recent years has been like living in darkness and someone turning the light on. It was as if we had seen the church, the Bible and God one particular way and then a genuine epiphany changed our perspectives of our faith. With solid biblical foundations, we now see mission as the organizing principle for the church. Once we grasped that, God sending his Son to earth made sense in ways that it had not before. It's not that hard a concept to understand, but it's a paradigm change with huge implications.

We reckon it's also not too hard to live out the implications. It's not rocket science. It's not brain surgery. As Hirsch reminds us with his teaching about missional DNA, it is within every believer, even if it is too often latent.[5]

Experimenting with being a missionary is not that difficult. If we can imagine a missional church as getting together a mob of Jesus followers and whoever else wants to join in, eating and worshiping together, and dreaming up how to serve a neighborhood and world around us, we do not need all the extras that usually come with church as we have inherited it. Michael Frost's book *Exiles* puts it in simple terms for us. He encourages anyone to give simple and diverse forms of missional church a go. Following Jesus in community,

listening to and praying for community needs and calling for a better
world do not require a university degree and three years of planning.
With the inspiration of Joseph the steward, who saved nations from
hunger, Daniel, who refused to eat junk served up to him, and Paul,
who ate to engage people rather than fearing contamination, Frost
caters a life-affirming and not-too-difficult approach to hospitality:
"Serve up something delicious, and then just watch the conversation
flow and trust God to stick his nose in somewhere."[6]

Sometimes the best evangelism happens when a Christian takes
time to do something he or she enjoys and does it with not-yet-
believers as part of sharing life. Similarly, the best missional initiatives can happen when we design a safe space for sharing life with
God and one another, and see who else wants to join us. Don't
worry about starting small with something new, but plan for growth,
be open to surprises, share some stories over food with appropriate
doses of laughter and prayer, invite people to experience God and
authentic community. Join in with what God is doing in the world,
and see what unfolds.[7]

Part of the beauty of sentness is you don't have to plan a whole
lot of modern infrastructure before you get started, or even after
you get started. You don't have to worry about the chaos of change
or feel like you have to manage and control it. You don't have to
stress about organizing everyone, as if it all depends on you as a
CEO-style leader telling everyone what to do. You can embrace the
shift to a new paradigm and flow with the rhythms of life. Hirsch
and Altclass explain this well in *The Forgotten Ways Handbook*:

> Planting a new church, or remissionalizing an existing one, in
> this approach isn't primarily about buildings, worship ser-
> vices, size of congregations, and pastoral care, but rather
> about gearing the whole community around natural disci-
> pling friendships, worship as lifestyle, and mission in the

context of everyday life. As a living network "in Christ" it can meet anywhere, anytime and still be a viable expression of church. This is a much more organic way to plant a church or to revitalize it.[8]

Does that capture your imagination in any way? If you could do anything and resources were not a limitation, we wonder what new thing you might start. What is the dangerous story you want to see unfold in your neighborhood?

TRIBES NEED YOU TO LEAD

Marketing guru Seth Godin's book *Tribes* helped us understand that in today's networked world, anyone can exercise leadership from anywhere and can bring together a group of like-minded people.[9] Online communication helps, but the key is someone who is prepared to connect with other people and help people connect together. You don't need to wait for permission. You don't need to collect all the resources and knowhow first. You don't need to worry about conflict. Fear of failure or blame or criticism holds lots of us back too often.

Encountering criticism because of experimentation is a badge of honor. It shows you are trying something and achieving some level of change. Get used to the discomfort, but also to the adventure of putting your flag in the ground, standing up for something, proposing an idea that might fail, challenging the status quo, working hard on the implications and refusing to settle for second best. Godin counsels not to hesitate in being remarkable and crazy, to recruit other passionate individuals looking for a cause and to lead with passion and generous empowerment. He shows that people want an adventurous journey, and they want to belong, help and serve. Leadership is not what others do but what any of us can do: "The secret of leadership is simple: Do what you believe in. Paint a picture of the future. Go there. People will follow."[10]

Scott Beale leads the diverse and innovative company Laughing Squid, which offers an eclectic range of services from web hosting to laser engraving. While attending a conference in 2008, he grew tired of lining up to get access to a Google party. Dissatisfied with the wait, he walked down the street to an empty bar and announced on Twitter, "Alta Vista Party at Ginger Man." Fifty people soon turned up. Twitter facilitated the communication, but it was Scott's tribal connections and his initiative, combined with an imagination-grabbing and timely idea, that gathered the tribe together. It was an Alta Vista party because he said it was, and he had the authority to declare it as such. He made something *ex nihilo*—out of nothing.[11]

Beale's party prompts us to ask, what tribal events we are inviting people to gather for? How do we plan and host those events? How flexible are we with meeting places and communicating plans? Does the church have an *ex nihilo* ministry? What does the church need at its disposal to make parties out of nothing? How can we cultivate the respect and permission of people that will allow them to start something new out of nothing?

START AND STAY GRASSROOTS

Missional imagination and practice is not that hard. We do encourage you, though, to stay close to the grassroots of mission. We ask ourselves where we often find the activity of God. Where is it that we find the kingdom of God being extended? From our experience, it is often at the edge of the church and the city, where we find those living on mission without fanfare or fuss.

Now let us clarify: there are always exceptions to rules and plenty of variations to every principle. God is active in all sorts of expressions of the church. However, time and time again we are inspired not by those at the center of power and influence but by those who serve and minister to the most forgotten.

There is no direct connection between responsibility in church

leadership and the fruitfulness of mission or the health of your
spirituality. So we are convinced it is not only refreshing but essential that we stay in contact with those on the margins of the
church. We want to keep rubbing shoulders with and hearing the
stories of those who are reaching out to others and involved in
God's redemptive plan for the world. And we want to stay a part of
that kind of grassroots ministry for the rest of our lives, as well as
to train and encourage others in those directions.

The more entrenched you get in church ministry, the more we
encourage you to stay connected to the ground, to the grassroots,
to the average person. This is part of what we love about Forge. It
can be fun to sit in high-caliber meetings. It can stroke the ego to
contribute to important-sounding committees. It can be stimu-
lating to hear stories from missional practitioners and be instructed
by thoughtful academic teachers. But if we have our hearts and
minds captured by a missional imagination, we will realize that the
real action happens as we cooperate in the mission of God at grassroots levels.

Most of the residents who go through Forge are moms and mechanics, artists and accountants, teachers and average workers.
Some are church planters or leaders of missional projects. But they
tend to be people who feel like square pegs in round holes in normal
church. Typical church infrastructures were not home to them.
When we imagine a missional church, we are in the best place when
we engage in grassroots mission.

For me (Kim), my wife, Maria, is the ultimate barometer of how
true we are to what we say. Forge has always said it trains and networks first in the arena of grassroots mission. Maria is not a sales-
person; she does not talk things up. Quite honestly she is my bucket
of cold water, as she regularly asks, "But how will that work?" I
remember being really happy when Maria and I went to the first
graduation of Forge Chicago residents. All of them were ordinary

people. None of them was paid Forge staff. Maria said, "This feels just like Australia."

Part of the genius of Forge's genesis in Australia was our focus on grassroots mission. Before missional was trendy, before Hirsch and Frost were the authors of several award-winning books, Forge started with a vision and ethos of resourcing the whole people of God as a sent people. Maria knew that. We are glad that this DNA continues as we expand in America and other national networks across the world. That is a good thing.

It's tempting to talk about the mission of God and the role that the church is to play in that mission, and then to go about our business. This is what we are taught to do in a consumer culture: spend our time in nothing except telling or hearing something new (Acts 17:21). But the kingdom of God is not a matter of talk but of power (1 Corinthians 4:20). The mission of God is not something to be consumed and then forgotten; it's something to be embraced and participated in.

Like we do in Forge training, we encourage you to start something new. Start and stay at the grassroots level. Through that we hope your life and outlook is changed for good and for God. We hope and pray God is pleased by what you do. After all the talking and books and blogs and tweets and Facebook updates about the tweets, God continues to bless us when somebody starts something new as a carrier of the good news. Start something new, or let something new start in you.

THE STORY OF EVERETT HOWARD

Over forty years ago, a young man prepared to live a dangerous story. He had a sense he was called to something but was not sure where God wanted to send him. One day he went into his family's church, locked the door so he could be alone and knelt down with a piece of paper and a pen. He had known God's call but was not sure where God wanted to send him or what God wanted him to do or when God wanted to send him. He wrote all that he was willing to do. He listed it all—reading the Bible, giving his offerings, serving in his church and being a missionary. The list included everything he thought God might require. It was a long list, and he meant it all.

When he finished writing, he signed his name at the bottom, laid the paper on the altar and waited for a sign of God's approval. He suspected God would be quite proud of him in his willingness to make this stand. But nothing transpired. He did not hear anything or feel any different. He was pretty disappointed. But then a thought struck him: maybe there was something he had forgotten. So he grabbed the paper and checked it, but there was nothing he could add.

After waiting for what felt like too long, he felt God speak to him in his spirit: "Son, you are going about this all wrong. Take the paper and tear it up." So he did. "Now take a fresh blank page, sign that at the bottom, and let me fill it."

And God did fill in the page of his life. Everett served for thirty-six years in the Cape Verde Islands. He was glad he had not known everything that would come—the fever he contracted three thousand miles from help, the famine during which he almost starved, the nine months when he had little money and sold everything to survive. All of that was on God's page, and Everett would not change a thing. And if he had to do it over, he would sign the blank page again and take every step.

Each of us has a story to write. Many of the pages are already filled, and we cannot change them, whether good or bad. But ahead of us is a blank page. Are you willing to sign the blank page and hand it to God? Say, "Here I am—the personality you gave me, the gifts you have granted me, my family, my money, my training, my dreams, my destiny. God, I want what you want." Do you want to write your story not independently but dependent on God? Not living just for yourself, but for God and for others? Not determining your own destiny but asking God to write an exciting and fulfilling life for you wherever God wants to send you?

God may have used you a lot, and you might feel in desperate need of refreshing. Or maybe you are just starting out in a life of sentness and feel eager to follow and learn. You might have a clear sense of guidance about where God will plant you, or you might feel overwhelmed by the possibilities. Whatever your situation, we encourage you that God is willing and able to send you into your world to write radical and dangerous stories of your own.

ACKNOWLEDGMENTS

THE BEST STORIES HAVE imagination-grabbing characters who rely on one another as a tribe or team in the face of danger. As writers and practitioners, an inspiring tribe of characters surrounds us.

Thank you to the life-giving and Jesus-inspired communities we have had the privilege of sharing life and mission with, especially AuburnLife and the broader Baptist Union of Victoria tribe for Darren, and The Junction and Community Christian Church for Kim. Our mentors and communities shape the people we are today and help us embrace our sentness.

I (Kim) would especially like to thank Steve Swain. You took a risk with me in sharing life and standing in the gap. I am a man of God today because of you.

Thanks to the crazy creative types we have journeyed within Forge for over a decade—staff, board members, teams, residents and interns who have inspired and taught us. We both love being a part of the Forge Mission Training Network; you are an amazing tribe of practitioners.

Thank you, Lance Ford, for overseeing the Forge America publishing line, and Dave Zimmerman, for championing and editing this book.

And thanks to our families, whom we most love sharing life with. Maria Hammond and Jenni Cronshaw, you inspire us and keep us down-to-earth. We owe you a ride in a hot-air balloon. And our children, Lachlan, Carter and Jordan Hammond, and Benjamin, Jessie and Emily Cronshaw, we are proud of you, and we look forward to the wild dreams and radical action with which you will change the world. In fact, you are already doing it.

One month after the Hammonds moved to Chicago in December 2009, as we were starting to dream about this book, seven year-old Carter was diagnosed with leukemia. Hundreds of treatments and transfusions later, Carter had his last chemotherapy March 24, 2013. He is facing life courageously, surrounded by love and care of his family and friends (see clippersforcarter.com).

In June 2013, as we were finishing *Sentness*, sixty-three-year-old Ross Langmead had a massive heart attack and died seven days later. Ross was a well-loved Baptist church leader and urban missionary in Melbourne, and one of Australia's foremost missiologists. He taught as professor of mission at Whitley College, was a friend and supporter of Forge and was Darren's research supervisor, academic mentor and friend. Ross's life embodied much of what is written here.

We proudly dedicate this book to Carter and the life he now has to live, wherever God sends him, and to Ross and the inspiration of his life—of sentness—well lived.

BEST FURTHER READING

Bosch, David J. *Transforming Mission: Paradigm Shifts in Theology of Mission*. Maryknoll, NY: Orbis, 1991.

Cole, Neil, and Phil Helfer. *Church Transfusion: Changing Your Church Organically—From the Inside Out*. San Francisco: Jossey-Bass, 2012.

Cray, Graham. *Mission-Shaped Church: Church Planting and Fresh Expressions of Church in a Changing Context*. London: Church House, 2004.

Ford, Lance. *Unleader: Reimagining Leadership . . . and Why We Must*. Kansas City, MO: Beacon Hill Press, 2012.

Ford, Lance, and Brad Brisco. *Missional Essentials*. Kansas City: House, 2012.

Ford, Lance, and Brad Brisco. *The Missional Quest: Becoming a Church of the Long Run*. Downers Grove, IL: InterVarsity Press, 2013.

Frost, Michael. *Exiles: Living Missionally in a Post-Christian Culture*. Peabody, MA: Hendrickson, 2006.

Frost, Michael. *Incarnate: The Body of Christ in an Age of Disengagement*. Downers Grove, IL: InterVarsity Press, 2014.

Frost, Michael, and Alan Hirsch. *The Shaping of Things to Come: Innovation and Mission for the 21st-Century Church*. Peabody, MA: Hendrickson, 2003.

Fryling, Robert A. *The Leadership Ellipse: Shaping How We Lead by Who We Are*. Downers Grove, IL: InterVarsity Press, 2010.

Guder, Darrell L., ed. *The Missional Church: A Vision for the Sending of the Church in North America*. Grand Rapids: Eerdmans, 1998.

Hirsch, Alan. *The Forgotten Ways: Reactivating the Missional Church*. Grand Rapids: Brazos, 2006.

Hirsch, Alan, with Darryn Altclass. *The Forgotten Ways Handbook: A Practical Guide for Developing Missional Churches*. Grand Rapids: Brazos, 2009.

Hirsch, Alan, and Lance Ford. *Right Here, Right Now: Everyday Mission for Everyday People*. Grand Rapids: Baker, 2011.

Holt, Simon Carey. *God Next Door: Spirituality & Mission in the Neighbourhood*. Brunswick East, Victoria: Acorn, 2007.

Nelson, Scott. Forge Guides for Missional Conversation. Downers Grove, IL: IVP Connect, 2013.

Richardson, Rick. *Reimagining Evangelism: Inviting Friends on a Spiritual Journey*. Downers Grove, IL: InterVarsity Press, 2006.

NOTES

Introduction: Shift

[1]Skip Blumberg, "'The Revolution Will Not Be Televised'—Gil Scott-Heron," interview, www.youtube.com/watch?v=kZvWt29OG0s.

[2]See Peter Kaldor et al., *Build My Church: Trends and Possibilities for Australian Churches* (Ashfield, NSW: OpenBook, 1999), pp. 50-58.

[3]Ralph D. Winter and Steven C. Hawthorne, eds., *Perspectives on the World Christian Movement: A Reader* (Pasadena: William Carey Library, 1981).

[4]Lesslie Newbigin, *Foolishness to the Greeks: The Gospel and Western Culture* (Geneva: WCC, 1986), p. 20.

[5]Lesslie Newbigin, *The Gospel in a Pluralist Society* (Grand Rapids: Eerdmans, 1989), p. 227.

[6]Michael Frost and Alan Hirsch, *The Shaping of Things to Come: Innovation and Mission for the 21st-Century Church* (Peabody, MA: Hendrickson, 2003); see also Darren Cronshaw, "The Shaping of Things Now: Mission and Innovation in Emerging Churches in Melbourne" (doctoral thesis, Melbourne College of Divinity, 2009), published as Darren Cronshaw, *The Shaping of Things Now: Emerging Church Mission and Innovation in 21st-Century Melbourne* (Saarbrücken, Germany: VDM Verlag, 2009). Read these and similar missional literature for perspectives on missional paradigms and where they are leading.

[7]Cronshaw, *Shaping of Things Now*, p. 45.

[8]See Lausanne Committee for World Evangelization, *The Lausanne Covenant: An Exposition and Commentary by John Stott* (Wheaton, IL: Lausanne Occasional Papers, no. 3, 1975).

[9]Alan Hirsch describes these different streams that he and Forge Mission Training Network draw from in his *The Forgotten Ways: Reactivating the Missional Church* (Grand Rapids: Brazos, 2006), pp. 269-70.

[10]Hirsch, *Forgotten Ways*, pp. 17, 71-72.

[11]Cronshaw, *Shaping of Things Now*, p. 10.

CHAPTER 1: BEYOND CONSUMERISM

[1]Drawing from Michael Frost and Alan Hirsch, *The Faith of Leap: Embracing a Theology of Risk, Adventure & Courage* (Grand Rapids: Baker Books, 2011); reviewed by Darren Cronshaw, "When Courage Counts—Frost and Hirsch Look at the Importance of the 'Leap of Faith' in Our Christian Walk," *Sight Magazine*, September 14, 2011, www.sightmagazine.com.au/stories/openbook/frost21.9.11.php.

[2]See Green Collect, www.greencollect.org.

[3]Eugene H. Peterson, *Working the Angles: The Shape of Pastoral Integrity* (Grand Rapids: Eerdmans, 1987), p. 2.

[4]See C. Christopher Smith, "Slow Down and Know That I Am God: Why It's Time for a Conversation About Slow Church," *Sojourners: Faith in Action for Social Justice*, December 2012, http://sojo.net/magazine/2012/12/slow-down-and-know-i-am-god; see also C. Christopher Smith and John Pattison, *Slow Church* (Downers Grove, IL: InterVarsity Press, 2014).

[5]Ray Simpson and Brent Lyons-Lee, *Emerging Downunder: Creating New Monastic Villages of God* (Adelaide: ATF, 2008), pp. 101-5.

[6]Drawing on Darren Cronshaw, *The Shaping of Things Now: Emerging Church Mission and Innovation in 21st-Century Melbourne* (Saarbrücken, Germany: VDM Verlag, 2009), pp. 107-21, 145-51, 193-94. Research and interview details are available in the book.

[7]Solace, www.solacechurch.org.au.

[8]Stuart Davey, ed., *Remaking: A Workbook for Spiritual Formation* (Melbourne: Solace EMC, 2006), pp. 18-19.

[9]George R. Hunsberger, "Sizing Up the Shape of the Church," in *The Church Between Gospel and Culture: The Emerging Mission in North America*, ed. George R. Hunsberger and Craig Van Gelder (Grand Rapids: Eerdmans, 1996), pp. 337-42.

[10]Davey, *Remaking*, p. 16.

[11]Future Travelers, www.futuretravelers.org; Alan Hirsch and Dave Ferguson, *On the Verge: A Journey into the Apostolic Future of the Church* (Grand Rapids: Zondervan, 2011), reviewed by Darren Cronshaw in *Sight Magazine*, "'Blue Ocean' Thinking About the Future of the Church,"

September 6, 2011, www.sightmagazine.com.au/stories/Books/hirsch28
.8.11.php.

[12]Lance Ford, *Unleader: Reimagining Leadership . . . and Why We Must* (Kansas City, MO: Beacon Hill Press, 2012).

CHAPTER 2: SENT PEOPLE

[1]Tim Dearborn, "Beyond Duty," in *Perspectives on the World Christian Movement: A Reader*, ed. Ralph D. Winter and Steven C. Hawthorne (Pasadena: William Carey Library, 2009), p. 70.

[2]We heard Australian evangelist Mal Garvin tell this story.

[3]Howard A. Snyder, *Liberating the Church: The Ecology of Church and Kingdom* (Downers Grove, IL: InterVarsity Press, 1983).

[4]David Bosch, *Transforming Mission: Paradigm Shifts in Theology of Mission* (Maryknoll, NY: Orbis, 1991), p. 390; discussed in Darren Cronshaw, *The Shaping of Things Now: Emerging Church Mission and Innovation in 21st-Century Melbourne* (Saarbrücken, Germany: VDM Verlag, 2009), pp. 39-40.

[5]Darrell L. Guder, ed., *The Missional Church: A Vision for the Sending of the Church in North America* (Grand Rapids: Eerdmans, 1998); see www
.gocn.org.

[6]Drawing on Cronshaw, *Shaping of Things Now*, pp. 89-106, 135-44, 185-89. See also www.urbanlife.otg.au.

[7]Michael Frost and Alan Hirsch, *The Shaping of Things to Come: Innovation and Mission for the 21st-Century Church* (Peabody, MA: Hendrickson, 2003), pp. 23-28.

[8]Brian D. McLaren, "Dorothy on Leadership or 'How a Movie from Childhood Can Help Us Understand the Changing Nature of Leadership in the Postmodern Tradition,'" *Rev Magazine,* November/December 2000, www
.brianmclaren.net/emc/archives/imported/dorothy-on-leadership.html.

[9]Michelle Van Loon, "God Called Me to Move to the Trailer Park: How the Forgotten Outskirts of Chicagoland Became One Woman's Mission Field," *Christianity Today*, August 3, 2012, www.christianitytoday.com/thisisourcity/7thcity/trailerpark.html.

[10]Ibid.

[11]Alan Roxburgh and M. Scott Boren, *Introducing the Missional Church: What It Is, Why It Matters, How to Become One* (Grand Rapids: Baker Books, 2009), p. 20.

¹²Ryan Hairston, email to Darren Cronshaw, May 2012.

¹³Ibid.

¹⁴The 2h Project, www.the2hproject.com.

CHAPTER 3: SUBMERGED MINISTRY

¹I (Kim) mentioned some of these experiences in my first stand-up comedy routine, "Kim Hammond at The Comedy Shrine Aurora," July 11, 2011, www.youtube.com/watch?v=D0sXCrDhUH0.

²Exponential: Accelerating Multiplication, www.exponential.org; see also NewThing, www.newthing.org.

³Interestingly, in the book that the movie is based on, the priest is her opponent, as he stands for traditional church teaching. Joanne Harris, *Chocolat* (London: Transworld, 1999).

⁴Michael Frost and Alan Hirsch, *ReJesus: A Wild Messiah for a Missional Church* (Peabody, MA: Hendrickson, 2009).

⁵See Michael Frost, *Exiles: Living Missionally in a Post-Christian Culture* (Peabody, MA: Hendrickson, 2006), p. 44.

⁶For exercises that aid a congregation in discerning where God is at work or what Jesus is brewing, see this practical and accessible guidebook on missional DNA and practices: Alan Hirsch with Darryn Altclass, *The Forgotten Ways Handbook: A Practical Guide for Developing Missional Churches* (Grand Rapids: Brazos, 2009).

⁷Cathleen Falsani, "Bono's American Prayer," *Christianity Today*, March 2003, www.christianitytoday.com/ct/2003/marchweb-only/2.38.html.

⁸Darren Cronshaw, "Dances with Locals," *W!tness: The Voice of Victorian Baptists*, May 2012, https://buv.com.au/witness-online/325-may12-dances-with-locals.

⁹Vincent J. Donovan, *Christianity Rediscovered* (Maryknoll, NY: Orbis, 1983), p. 41; discussed in Darren Cronshaw, *Credible Witness: Companions, Prophets, Hosts and Other Australian Mission Models* (Melbourne: Urban Neighbours of Hope, 2006), pp. 73-74.

¹⁰Rick Richardson, *Reimagining Evangelism: Inviting Friends on a Spiritual Journey* (Queensway, UK: Scripture Union, 2006). We thank Naomi Swindon for pointing us to these helpful images.

¹¹Brian Sanders, *Life After Church: God's Call to Disillusioned Christians* (Downers Grove, IL: InterVarsity Press, 2007).

[12]The Underground, "Our Manifesto," tampaundergound.com/our-manifesto.

[13]Michael Banes, "Pulpit to Fire Station," 2012, http://soundcloud.com/story team/michael-pulpit-to-fire-station.

[14]Philip Freier, "A New Willingness to Connect," in *Facing the Future: Bishops Imagine a Different Church*, ed. Stephen Hale and Andrew Curnow (Brunswick East, Victoria: Acorn, 2009), p. 221; reviewed by Darren Cronshaw in *Australian Journal of Mission Studies* 5, no. 1 (June 2011): 84, 27.

[15]Simon Carey Holt, *God Next Door: Spirituality & Mission in the Neighbourhood* (Brunswick East, Victoria: Acorn, 2007); discussed in Darren Cronshaw, "Reenvisioning Theological Education and Missional Spirituality," *Journal of Adult Theological Education* 9, no. 1 (2012): 9-27.

[16]Michael Frost, "Adopt a Posture of Listening," Verge Conference, Austin, Texas, April 2012, www.youtube.com/watch?v=v2TtyIQ3ous.

[17]See also Sherry and Geoff Maddock, "An Ever-Renewed Adventure of Faith: Notes from a Community," in *An Emergent Manifesto of Hope*, ed. Doug Pagitt and Tony Jones (Grand Rapids: Baker Books, 2007), pp. 79-88.

Cʜᴀᴘᴛᴇʀ 4: Sʜᴀʟᴏᴍ Sᴘɪʀɪᴛᴜᴀʟɪᴛʏ

[1]Cornelius Plantinga, *Not the Way It's Supposed to Be: A Breviary of Sin* (Grand Rapids: Eerdmans, 1995), p. 10.

[2]Messianic spirituality is introduced in Michael Frost and Alan Hirsch, *The Shaping of Things to Come: Innovation and Mission for the 21st-Century Church* (Peabody, MA: Hendrickson, 2003), pp. 111-62, and discussed in Darren Cronshaw, *The Shaping of Things Now: Emerging Church Mission and Innovation in 21st-Century Melbourne* (Saarbrücken, Germany: VDM Verlag, 2009), pp. 36-69. The following pages draw on our Forge teaching of spirituality, sustainability and discipleship as outlined in Darren Cronshaw, "Reenvisioning Theological Education and Missional Spirituality," *Journal of Adult Theological Education* 9, no. 1 (2012): 9-27.

[3]Alan Hirsch with Darryn Altclass, *The Forgotten Ways Handbook: A Practical Guide for Developing Missional Churches* (Grand Rapids: Brazos, 2009), p. 95.

[4]Roger Helland and Leonard Hjalmarson, *Missional Spirituality: Embodying God's Love from the Inside Out* (Downers Grove, IL: InterVarsity Press, 2011), p. 28.

[5]Nancy Reeves, *Spirituality for Extroverts (and Tips for Those Who Love Them)* (Nashville: Abingdon, 2008); reviewed by Darren Cronshaw, in *W!tness: The Voice of Victorian Baptists* 91, no. 8 (September 2011): 9.

[6]Ross Langmead, "Theological Reflection in Ministry and Mission," *Ministry Society and Theology* 18 (2004): 25-26; drawing on Donald Messer, *Contemporary Images of Christian Ministry* (Nashville: Abingdon, 1989); discussed in Darren Cronshaw, "Reenvisioning Theological Education, Mission and the Local Church," *Mission Studies* 28, no. 1 (June 2011): 91-115.

[7]Langmead, "Theological Reflection," pp. 12-13; see also his website, www.rosslangmead.com.

[8]Alan Hirsch and Dave Ferguson, *On the Verge: A Journey into the Apostolic Future of the Church* (Grand Rapids: Zondervan, 2011).

[9]See Jonathan Wilson-Hartgrove, *The Wisdom of Stability* (Brewster, MA: Paraclete Press, 2010).

[10]Eugene H. Peterson, *The Contemplative Pastor: Returning to the Art of Spiritual Direction* (Grand Rapids: Eerdmans, 1989), p. 12.

[11]For a fuller reflection on Luke 10 and its radical missional implications, see Alan Roxburgh, *Missional: Joining God in the Neighborhood* (Grand Rapids: Baker, 2011), pp. 115-78.

[12]Tim Costello, *Hope: Moments of Inspiration in a Challenging World* (Melbourne: Hardie Grant, 2012), pp. 207-8.

[13]N. T. Wright, *Surprised by Hope* (New York: HarperOne, 2008), pp. 111, 211-15, 236.

[14]Marie Dennis, *Saint Francis* (Maryknoll, NY: Orbis, 2002), p. 40.

[15]Thomas Merton, *Contemplative Prayer* (London: Darton, Longman & Todd, 1969), p. 23.

[16]Richard Rohr, *The Naked Now: Learning to See How the Mystics See* (New York: Crossroad, 2009), p. 180.

[17]Simone Weil, *Waiting for God*, trans. Emma Craufurd (New York: Harper Perennial, 1951), p. 57.

[18]Eugene H. Peterson, *Working the Angles: The Shape of Pastoral Integrity* (Grand Rapids: Eerdmans, 1987), pp. 3-4.

[19]Ibid., p. 40.

[20]Frost and Hirsch, *Shaping*, p. 126.

[21]Ibid., p. 116.

[22]Helland and Hjalmarson, *Missional Spirituality*, pp. 142-52, 198-210.

[23]Drawing on Cronshaw, *Shaping of Things Now*, pp. 70-88, 129-35. See also Eastern Hills Community Church, www.ehillschurch.com.

[24]N. T. Wright, *Jesus and the Victory of God* (London: SPCK, 1996), esp. pp. 198-226.

[25]Cronshaw, *Shaping of Things Now*, p. 131.

[26]M. Robert Mulholland Jr., *Invitation to a Journey: A Road Map for Spiritual Formation* (Downers Grove, IL: InterVarsity Press, 1993), p. 15, emphasis added.

[27]Robert E. Webber, *The Divine Embrace* (Grand Rapids: Baker, 2010), p. 160, emphasis added.

CHAPTER 5: SAFE PLACES

[1]For Debra Hirsch's treatment of sexuality, see her *Sex, Grace and Truth* (Downers Grove, IL: InterVarsity Press, 2014).

[2]Jon Owen, *Muddy Spirituality: Bringing It All Down to Earth* (Dandenong: UNOH Publishing, 2011), p. 134.

[3]Ibid.

[4]Tim Winton, *Cloudstreet* (Ringwood: Penguin, 1992).

[5]Andrew Denton, "Tim Winton," *Enough Rope with Andrew Denton*, October 25, 2004, www.abc.net.au/tv/enoughrope/transcripts/s1227915 .htm. We appreciate Paul Cameron pointing us to this episode in his article "Rediscovering Balance," *Reo: A Journal of Theology and Ministry* 35, no. 1 (2009): 23-26.

[6]Tim Winton, *The Turning* (Sydney: Picador, 2004), pp. 133-61. We appreciate Douglas Hynd pointing out this story in his article "Getting Back to Jesus? Theology, Mission and Christendom," *Australian Journal of Mission Studies* 2, no. 2 (2008): 67-68.

[7]John Drane, *The McDonaldization of the Church: Spirituality, Creativity and the Future of the Church* (London: Darton, Longman & Todd, 2000).

[8]See Eddie Gibbs and Ian Coffey, *ChurchNext: Quantum Changes in Christian Ministry* (Leicester, UK: Inter-Varsity Press, 2001), pp. 198-206.

[9]David Tacey, *The Spirituality Revolution: The Emergence of Contemporary Spirituality* (Sydney: HarperCollins, 2003), p. 194.

[10]Rick Richardson, *Reimagining Evangelism: Inviting Friends on a Spiritual Journey* (Queensway, UK: Scripture Union, 2007), pp. 41-43.

[11]Rick Richardson, *Evangelism Outside the Box: New Ways to Help People Expe-*

rience the Good News (Downers Grove, IL: InterVarsity Press, 2000), p. 48.

[12]Alan Jamieson, *A Churchless Faith: Faith Journey Beyond the Churches* (London: SPCK, 2002), pp. 119-34, 158-62; James W. Fowler, *Stages of Faith: The Psychology of Human Development and the Quest for Meaning* (San Francisco: Harper, 1995).

[13]Ajith Fernando, "The Uniqueness of Jesus Christ," in *Telling the Truth: Evangelizing Postmoderns*, ed. D. A. Carson (Grand Rapids: Zondervan, 2000), p. 133.

[14]Colin Smith, "The Ambassador's Job Description; 2 Corinthians 5:11-21," in *Telling the Truth*, p. 183.

[15]Michael Frost and Alan Hirsch, *The Shaping of Things to Come: Innovation and Mission for the 21st-Century Church* (Peabody, MA: Hendrickson, 2003), pp. 47-50, 206-10; Darren Cronshaw, *The Shaping of Things Now: Emerging Church Mission and Innovation in 21st-Century Melbourne* (Saarbrücken, Germany: VDM Verlag, 2009), p. 54.

[16]See Solace's experience in Cronshaw, *Shaping of Things Now*, p. 172; Olivia Moffat, "What Kind of Church?" Evangelical Fellowship in the Anglican Communion (EFAC) National Leadership Consultation, 2011, http://home.vicnet.net.au/~efac/whatchurch.htm.

[17]These are estimated figures of those age twelve and over in 2010. Substance Abuse and Mental Health Services Administration, *Results from the 2010 National Survey on Drug Use and Health: Summary of National Findings*, NSDUH Series H-41, HHS Publication No. (SMA) 11-4658 (Rockville, MD: Substance Abuse and Mental Health Services Administration, 2011), www.samhsa.gov/data/NSDUH/2k10ResultsRev/NS-DUHresultsRev2010.htm.

[18]National Council on Problem Gambling, "FAQs—Problem Gamblers," www.ncpgambling.org/i4a/pages/index.cfm?pageid=3390.

[19]Michael Leahy, *Porn Nation: Conquering America's #1 Addiction* (Chicago: Northfield, 2008).

[20]Ryan Hairston, email to Darren Cronshaw, June 18, 2012.

[21]Mercy Street, www.mercystreet.org; Sean Gladding, "What the Church Can Learn from Addicts and Drunks" (paper presented at Exponential, Orlando, Florida, September 2012); Sean Gladding, email to Darren Cronshaw, November 20, 2012.

[22]Jerome Ellison, *Report to the Creator: A Spiritual Biography of Our Era* (New York: Harper & Brothers, 1955).

[23]Adapted from Darren Cronshaw, "Being Church for Curious Visitors," *W!tness: The Voice of Victorian Baptists* 91, no. 6 (August 2011): 8.

[24]Told by Greg Hunt, Forge El Paso director, via Ryan Hairston, email to Darren Cronshaw, June 18, 2012.

[25]Rusty is talking about Malcolm Willis, a missional leader in Bradford, England, who runs a pub called the Cock & Bottle as a place where the gospel can intersect people's daily lives. His story is told in Frost and Hirsch, *Shaping of Things to Come,* pp. 10-11.

CHAPTER 6: SHARED LIFE

[1]Gilbert Bilezikian, *Community 101: Reclaiming the Local Church as Community of Oneness* (Grand Rapids: Zondervan, 1997).

[2]Michael Leunig, *When I Talk to You: A Cartoonist Talks to God* (Pymble, NSW: HarperCollins, 2004).

[3]See Gordon Macdonald, *When Men Think Private Thoughts* (Nashville: Thomas Nelson, 1996), pp. 96-98.

[4]Steve Biddulph, *Manhood: An Action Plan for Changing Men's Lives* (Sydney: Finch Publishing, 1995), p. 305.

[5]From Susan S. Phillips, "The Practices of Friendship: Learning from Jesus, Martha and Mary," *Radix* 23, no. 4: 4-7, 26.

[6]Alan Hirsch and Dave Ferguson, *On the Verge: A Journey into the Apostolic Future of the Church* (Grand Rapids: Zondervan, 2011), pp. 194-95.

[7]Nancy C. Lutkehaus, *Margaret Mead: The Making of an American Icon* (Princeton, NJ: Princeton University Press, 2008), p. 4.

[8]Dietrich Bonhoeffer, *Life Together* (London: SCM, 1954), pp. 15-16.

[9]Robert A. Fryling, *The Leadership Ellipse: Shaping How We Lead by Who We Are* (Downers Grove, IL: InterVarsity Press, 2010), p. 131.

CHAPTER 7: STANDING IN THE GAP

[1]This section draws on Darren Cronshaw, "New Age Partnerships Proposed," *The Victorian Baptist Witness,* July 1997, p. 18; Hugh Mackay, *Generations: Baby Boomers, Their Parents and Their Children* (Sydney: Macmillan, 1997).

[2]Darren Cronshaw, *The Shaping of Things Now: Emerging Church Mission and Innovation in 21st-Century Melbourne* (Saarbrücken, Germany: VDM Verlag, 2009), p. 185.

[3]This section draws on Cronshaw, *Shaping of Things Now*, pp. 121-22, 145-47, 193-95; Solace, www.solacechurch.org.au.

[4]Barb Totterdell, "Edge of Chaos Solace" (class paper, Ridley College, 2004).

[5]Neil Cole, *Organic Church: Growing Faith Where Life Happens* (San Francisco: Jossey-Bass, 2005), p. 215; reviewed by Darren Cronshaw in *W!tness: The Voice of Victorian Baptists* 89, no. 6 (July 2009): 20. See also Church Multiplication Associates, www.cmaresources.org.

[6]Neil Cole and Phil Helfer, *Church Transfusion: Changing Your Church Organically—From the Inside Out* (San Francisco: Jossey-Bass, 2012); reviewed by Darren Cronshaw in *Australian eJournal of Theology* 20, no. 2 (2013).

[7]Stuart Murray, *Changing Mission: Learning from the Newer Churches* (London: Churches Together in Britain and Ireland, 2006); reviewed by Darren Cronshaw in *W!tness: The Voice of Victorian Baptists* 89, no. 6 (2009): 21.

[8]Graham Cray, *Mission-Shaped Church: Church Planting and Fresh Expressions of Church in a Changing Context* (London: Church House, 2004).

[9]See her first appearance at "Susan Boyle—Britains Got Talent 2009 Episode 1—Saturday 11th April," www.youtube.com/watch?v=RxPZh4AnWyk. Her first CD was titled *I Dreamed a Dream*.

CONCLUSION: STARTING SOMETHING NEW

[1]Mark Scandrette, "Growing Pains: The Messy and Fertile Process of Becoming," in *An Emergent Manifesto of Hope*, ed. Doug Pagitt and Tony Jones (Grand Rapids: Baker Books, 2007), pp. 22-32.

[2]Frederick Buechner, *Wishful Thinking: A Theological ABC* (New York: Harper & Row, 1973), p. 95.

[3]Quoted in Michael Frost and Alan Hirsch, *The Shaping of Things to Come: Innovation and Mission for the 21st-Century Church* (Peabody, MA: Hendrickson, 2003), pp. 185-89; discussed in Darren Cronshaw, *The Shaping of Things Now: Emerging Church Mission and Innovation in 21st-Century Melbourne* (Saarbrücken, Germany: VDM Verlag, 2009), p. 66.

[4]Drawing on Alan Hirsch and Dave Ferguson, *On the Verge: A Journey into the Apostolic Future of the Church* (Grand Rapids: Zondervan, 2011).

[5]Alan Hirsch with Darryn Altclass, *The Forgotten Ways Handbook: A Practical Guide for Developing Missional Churches* (Grand Rapids: Brazos, 2009).

[6]Michael Frost, *Exiles: Living Missionally in a Post-Christian Culture* (Peabody, MA: Hendrickson, 2006), p. 168; reviewed by Darren Cronshaw in *Zadok Perspectives* 96 (Spring 2007): 24-25.

[7]Michael Riddell, Mark Pierson and Cathy Kirkpatrick, *The Prodigal Project: Journey into the Emerging Church* (London: SPCK, 2001); reviewed in Darren Cronshaw, "The Emerging Church: Introductory Reading Guide," *Zadok Papers* S143 (Summer 2005): 15.

[8]Hirsch and Altclass, *Forgotten Ways*, p. 185.

[9]Seth Godin, *Tribes: We Need You to Lead Us* (New York: Portfolio, 2008); reviewed by Darren Cronshaw in *Crucible* 3, no. 1 (2010), www.ea.org.au/Crucible/Issues/Seth-Godin-Tribes-We-Need-You-to-Lead-Us-Portfolio-2008.aspx.

[10]Ibid., p. 108.

[11]Ibid., pp. 37-38.

Forge

The Forge Missions Training Network exists to help birth and nurture the missional church in America and beyond. Books published by Inter-Varsity Press that bear the Forge imprint will also serve that purpose.

Creating a Missional Culture, by JR Woodward

Forge Guides for Missional Conversation (set of five), by Scott Nelson

Incarnate, by Michael Frost

The Missional Quest, by Lance Ford and Brad Brisco

More Than Enchanting, by Jo Saxton

Sentness, by Kim Hammond and Darren Cronshaw

The Story of God, the Story of Us (book and DVD), by Sean Gladding

---

For more information on Forge America, to apply for a Forge residency, or to find or start a Forge hub in your area, visit **www.forgeamerica.com**

For more information about Forge books from InterVarsity Press, including forthcoming releases, visit **www.ivpress.com/forge**